Heaven's Gold

Resurrecting Faith in
Today's Youth

David McMurtry

WestBow
PRESS
A DIVISION OF THOMAS NELSON

WestBow Press books may be ordered through booksellers or by contacting:

WestBow Press
A Division of Thomas Nelson
1663 Liberty Drive
Bloomington, IN 47403
www.westbowpress.com
1-(866) 928-1240

ISBN: 978-1-4497-8726-4 (sc)
ISBN: 978-1-4497-8725-7 (e)
ISBN: 978-1-4497-8727-1 (hc)

Library of Congress Control Number: 2013904088

Printed in the United States of America

WestBow Press rev. date: 5/23/2013

Scripture taken from the King James Version of the Bible.
Scripture quotations are from The Holy Bible, English Standard Version® (ESV®), copyright © 2001 by Crossway, a publishing ministry of Good News Publishers. Used by permission. All rights reserved.
Scriptures taken from the Holy Bible, New International Version®, NIV®. Copyright © 1973, 1978, 1984, 2011 by Biblica, Inc.™ Used by permission of Zondervan. All rights reserved worldwide. www.zondervan.com The "NIV" and "New International Version" are trademarks registered in the United States Patent and Trademark Office by Biblica, Inc.™ All rights reserved.

CONTENTS

PREFACE

Several years ago while sitting in a Bible study class, our teacher mentioned a study he had seen stating that a vast majority of children were leaving the church as they went off to college. That seemed preposterous at the time but as I thought more about it and did my own research about this phenomenon, not only was it plausible, it was becoming an epidemic problem in the church.

It has taken the church a long time to admit the obvious, but it is no longer a given that young people will continue in the religious footsteps of their parents and grandparents. While spending the last six years researching and writing "Heaven's Gold", I have investigated why kids are leaving the church as well as what it will take to resurrect their faith by interviewing dozens of people on the front line of this assault on their faith. Inspiration for this writing came from watching needless struggles of faith in the church, simply because of how we currently teach the Bible. The intent is to help the church realize the magnitude of young people leaving the church and to provide a foolproof way of bringing them back. The more I learned about the dynamics of this loss of faith among our youth, the more inspired I was to do something about it.

My job puts me on the road approximately 1,000-1,200 hours per year. This allows time for intense Bible study and scrutiny of Scripture, which is how this method of teaching the Bible was formulated. When you think about it, if we were to tithe our time in Bible study, we could study through the entire

Bible every month. As it is, my goal is to study through the Bible at least ten times each year while memorizing various books of the Bible along the way. My formula for Bible study is pretty simple: I check my faith, religion, doctrine and preconceived ideas at the door so that each time I walk through the Bible, it is as fresh as the first time I ever read it. Although I typically fly to distant destinations while on business, more times than I can count I have driven from Nashville to Tampa or Dallas or other cities about ten hours away for quick meetings and then drive back the next day. This allows me to study through the New Testament in less than 48 hours on those trips, which illuminates aspects of Scripture from a different perspective. I have also presented books of the Bible to church and college groups from memory as well as presented Paul's second letter to Timothy in Spanish in full first century prison attire from the depth of Paul's emotions. I don't consider the Bible a religious book at all. To me, it is a treasure map for finding spiritual gold and having an abundant, Spirit-filled life beyond our imagination which glorifies our God and Creator.

This book is principally targeted at parents and adults since it shows how the faith of their precious children can thrive in this spiritually hostile environment by transforming the way we teach the Bible. It is also written to teenagers and young adults who are or may one day struggle with their faith as it presents a fresh interpretation of Scripture. "Heaven's Gold" leads the reader on an interactive treasure hunt through Scripture, leaving no stone or clue unturned as it encourages its readers to look at the Bible through the eyes of a teenager struggling to believe. There will be some clues on this Scripture safari that people who have gone to church all of their lives may have trouble deciphering as they venture through the terrain our young people face every day. If churches will follow the game plan outlined in "Heaven's Gold", the faith of young people will come alive again as the church is transformed more closely into what Jesus intended it to be.

I want to thank my incredible wife, Kathy, for her enormous help of editing as well as being a sounding board for some of the things presented. Without her help, this book could have never been written. I appreciate my family's support which has made this journey through the Bible a labor of love.

CHAPTER 1

Treasure Hunt

Near the end of the movie *National Treasure*, Nicolas Cage and his associates stumbled upon what they thought was the treasure they had been seeking. After following clue after clue from ancient writings, they had tried to find a great treasure, although they weren't really sure of its size or location or whether it actually existed. After enduring twists and turns followed by dead ends that led to more twists and turns and dead ends, they approached a room they hoped would reveal a hidden bounty. As they walked into an empty treasure room, it hit them that they may have been chasing a pipe dream—just stories passed along through the centuries. When it dawned on them that there might have been yet another clue left to unravel, they finally reached what they sought: a room filled with so much treasure that it could barely be counted. As their mouths dropped open, the scene revealed mountains of gold and ancient artifacts worth billions.

That resembles the treasure hunt people in the church have been on for centuries. The emotions of writers of ancient Scripture saturate the pages of the Bible, revealing clues of an enormous treasure there for the taking by anyone who is able to decipher its clues. The pens of these inspired writers were on fire, fueled by their passion to share their piece of the treasure map with those following in their footsteps. They spoke from the depths of their souls about people who risked everything in pursuit of the treasure like David's life-or-death encounter with a giant as well as Abraham's leap of faith into a new and hostile land. They also shared the heartbreaking consequences of those chasing the treasure in the wrong direction, making its acquisition impossible.

The forty or so writers inspired to chronicle their journey were not just eyewitnesses to these events. They were also part of the tapestry of their own stories as the echoes of loved ones lost resonated through their inspired words. The words of Scripture are pigmented by the emotions of treasure hunters called to record stories and events of triumph and tragedy to illuminate the road to take as well as which ones to avoid.

As such, the Bible is not just an old book of religious stories or a binding of rules and regulations to collect dust on a coffee table. The Bible is a treasure map pointing toward spiritual gold in quantities so great that they could envelop the world and change the dynamics of life on earth for the rest of time. Its stories are told by prophets and apostles and penned by those inspired by the same God we serve. Each of them gave their all and left their piece of the treasure map for generations to come to interpret and decode. Unfortunately, the treasure's coordinates still remain a mystery for many of us who are now trying to follow its clues.

Anytime a national lottery reaches such a staggering amount that it dominates the news, each of us has probably entertained thoughts imagining what it would be like to actually hit the lottery or sweepstakes. We may have daydreamed about what it would be like to have so much money that we could do anything for ourselves as well as the people around us to make the world a better place. Of course, the odds of that happening are incredibly small. The allure of having fame and fortune throughout history has driven many people to do foolish things, to the detriment of themselves and their families.

Deep down inside, we all may be looking for some kind of treasure; the fact that people still seek it means that we haven't yet found it. Whether it is spiritual or monetary currency, its value as well as its ease and certainty of acquisition will predicate our level of investment. For example, if a person came to your house and told you that a treasure was buried in your backyard and pointed to its location, three questions would likely come to mind: how much is the treasure worth, how hard is it to get, and how much faith do you have in the person who told you about it? You might be willing to grab a shovel to dig down a couple of feet for a thousand dollars, but you would not likely expend the energy required to dig ten feet down to find a five-dollar bill. So how far down would you dig to find billions? Christians are called upon to ask themselves every day what they think the treasure of God is worth and how much they are willing to invest to have it.

In Christianity we always talk about the treasure of God, but no one seems to be able to put his or her hands on it. Every Sunday in churches around the world, people will come together to talk about the treasure and its pursuit in their lives. They will pray about it and sing songs of praise proclaiming its worth and their hope of one day having it. They will discuss it in Bible classes, and they will tell their children stories about the treasure and its importance. No matter how many times it is discussed, prayed, or sung about, however, its location remains a mystery for most of the people seeking it. In every treasure hunt, people will eventually give up and settle for something less when the investment and uncertainty exceeds the perceived value. For the church today, that describes young people who are leaving the church, having given up the chase for the treasure of God.

The Elephant in the Room

For those who aren't aware of the magnitude of this phenomenon, the exodus of young people from the church seems like nothing the church has ever seen before. Young people are leaving the church in staggering numbers because they either think the treasure of God we talk about every Sunday doesn't exist or that it doesn't have much value for them. After all, nobody just walks away from a treasure.

How can kids go to church their entire lives but then run away from God as fast as they can once they are free to do so? That happens for one of these two reasons: either the Bible is not powerful enough and pertinent enough to sustain the faith of today's young people or we are teaching the Bible's truths the wrong way. It is one or the other. How in the world can something so strong and so powerful be so ineffective? How can something so valuable be discarded by those who could benefit from it the most?

Because God is certainly not the problem, the process of elimination tells us young people leave the religion of their youth because of the way we interpret the Bible—the map leading to God's treasure. As it is, young people are not just walking away as they go off to college or go live on their own. They are

being driven away by a religion set in its rigidity, havir
no significant adjustment to its theology or ability to inter
the treasure map for nearly two thousand years. Jesus' teachings
are timeless; the methods by which they are taught are not, or at
least they ought not be unchanging, regardless of the times.

Young people to some degree have left the church throughout
history but not on the scale that is happening in this generation.
The absence of faith in the things being taught drives people
away from the church, which is to say that kids are not buying
the things being taught. Although church leaders are well aware
of the problem, nobody wants to talk about it. It is the elephant
in the room. Churches go about their business every Sunday as
if nothing is wrong. Especially among families whose teenagers
have already left the church, the elephant sits with us in the pews
while we sing and pray and listen to the sermon.

As I researched the causes of young people leaving the
church, I have interviewed leaders of various churches and youth
groups in different cities and states. On one flight to Texas,
I happened to sit beside a sales professional with a religious
publishing company. During our conversation, she told me about
a young lady in her congregation who, while in high school, was
a very devout Christian with a great singing voice. But when this
teenager went off to college, she lost her faith and wasn't sure
what she believed anymore. Although the details would change,
this kind of story was repeated by church leaders about students
in their congregation all across the country. Young people aren't
vanishing because they are mad at something or someone; that
would be fixable. They just slip away as soon as the decision
about church attendance is truly theirs to make and not just
something their parents force them to do.

We would all like to think the elephant would leave on its own, but it will not. Even though not all young people are leaving the faith, the question becomes what is an acceptable loss? Although Jesus' illustration about lost sheep wasn't about percentages, he did note that a 1 percent loss was unacceptable. That would mean if we were losing only 3 percent of young adults, we should sit in sackcloth and ashes and bemoan our failure to properly teach the Bible. Unfortunately, the erosion of faith in the church of its young people seems to be far greater than that.

An Internet search related to young people leaving the church reveals numerous studies conducted by various organizations and from various perspectives in the past few years attempting to quantify the scope and magnitude of the problem. The very fact that these studies and polls have been commissioned highlights the realization by church leaders that an erosion of faith among young people is real and that it is snowballing in the wrong direction. Although the statistics vary between studies related to denomination, dogma, and life experience, it isn't hard to make the case from these studies that more than half of the church's young people might abandon their faith when they move away from home and break the siphon of the religion in which they were raised.

The irony is that typically none of this information is ever shared from the pulpit or in the church bulletin as a means of assisting families trying to resurrect the dead or dying faith of a loved one. Churches rejoice whenever new members join their congregation but the loss of faith of any of its teenagers at college tends to get swept under the rug and never spoken about except in whispers among its members. The fact that churches go about

their religious business and ritualistic activities wi
thinking about sending a spiritual search party defies

Have you ever wondered why the spiritual assaul,
particular generation is so much greater than what any generation
before it had experienced? The answer to that question is the
Internet's involvement in today's world. The Internet exposes
the inconsistencies of the lessons taught in our Sunday schools
as scrutiny among college students becomes the norm rather
than the exception. Like it or not, there is no question about
Christianity that is off limits for examination on-line. The
Internet has become a conduit for questioning anything about
everything, and religion has become fair game for this kind of
scrutiny.

There are numerous websites that debate biblical and
theological topics, and the majority of participants on these
websites seem to be students, presumably of college age. It
boggles my mind to think about where some of the ideas being
discussed are derived. I have seen threads of dialog for hundreds
of topics that probably weren't even considered fifty years ago.
Although much of what I have seen could not stand up to any
reasonable scrutiny, it doesn't have to. Many of these topics find
their way onto college campuses, with incoming freshmen being
the most vulnerable targets for off-beat theology. The problem
is that since the church has not encouraged or invited scrutiny
of the things it teaches, the first exposure to religious crossfire
these freshmen may face comes from shade-tree theologians in
the student center, dorm room or even in their classrooms.

Another disconnect generated by the Internet is related to
topics of faith. It is fair to ask what Christians have to believe
about the Bible. Of course, the first thought that crosses our

minds is that we have to believe everything in the Bible; that is a natural reaction. However, if young people are not allowed to question anything presented in the Bible, then all it takes to kill their faith is to break just one of the weakest links in the chain that fortifies faith in the Bible's teachings. In that regard, the Internet is relentless.

This might not be an issue if the church had encouraged an examination of the things it has taught throughout the course of time, and especially today before these teenagers go off to college. Since they have never been taught how to deflect those arrows of opposition, they are left to fend for themselves. Ultimately, that is one of the reasons their faith dies. The best time to prepare young minds for the spiritual assault they will face at college is while they are still with us. Because that is not happening, it is as if we are sending our young people to storm the spiritual beaches of Normandy but arming them only with butter knives.

The media is also another venue highlighting the problem of church exodus. I recently stumbled upon a television show whose dominant theme was that America is now in a post-Christian era. If this doesn't make us wake up and shake in our boots, it should. We all know the power the media has in our society. In today's world, the media tries to brain wash us into what it wants us to believe which is particularly evident in the social and political arena. It doesn't matter if we agree with this premise or not, if we cannot quantify to our youth the value and benefits of living within the envelope of God's power then we will continue to lose them in masses.

Let's think together for a minute. See if any of the leaders in your church can intelligently answer any of these simple questions:

- What are the coordinates of heaven and he'
- Biologically speaking, how exactly does the come upon a person?
- Did God physically take a walk in the garden ᴏɪ ⸌⸌ by putting one foot in front of the other?
- If God did not know whether Abraham would sacrifice Isaac until Abraham raised his knife to kill him, does that mean God is not actually omniscient?
- What defines God as male?
- If God is in us, are we in heaven?
- Biologically and metaphysically, how does Satan try to control seven billion people at the same time?

Typically, nobody will be able to answer any of these questions in a way that will promote faith or even make sense. I actually had a leader in the church try to answer the above question about Abraham by surmising that maybe God hid the answer from Himself. This sounds like a parent trying to explain how Santa Claus gets inside of houses without chimneys.

On the Internet and at colleges, hundreds of questions just like these are raised while our youth experience the religion of Christianity unable to venture satisfying answers. Peter fell victim to the same scrutiny by the high priest's servant while he and the elephant warmed themselves by the fire. If this could happen to Peter, who had been with Jesus just a few hours earlier, how difficult is it for teenagers to maintain their faith in this Internet age?

Whether we do it ourselves or let the world do it for us, the things the church teaches will be tested in the fire of believability by this generation and only those things that can survive this ype of examination can augment our children's faith. Many sink into the quicksand of uncertainty the world creates because it leads them in directions different than the way the church explained it.

Had we properly prepared them for this expedition, their faith would thrive. When scientific discoveries are made which cause the religious tectonic plates to shift from the knowledge of those discoveries, the church must allow its interpretation of Scripture to shift as well, as more of God's power and nature are revealed. Otherwise, the chasm between the two will become so large that young people will be unable to make the leap of faith between what can be explained and what cannot.

For centuries whenever the church could not answer questions about God, heaven and hell, the Holy Spirit, dinosaurs, or Satan, it tried to dismiss the matter by stating that "there are some things we weren't meant to know". If a science teacher tried to answer a student's question that way, their employment would be short-lived. Any question the church chooses not to answer, the world and the Internet will. In effect, we are giving the Internet the first shot at the hearts and minds of these teenagers. Therein lies the problem.

Lessons from Oz

Based on the tens of thousands of hours I have spent studying Scripture and reading through the Bible, my opinion is that the way the church is teaching God's Word is ultimately driving these young people away. There are several fatal flaws in the way the Bible is taught in churches today that make it impossible for the treasure to be found. God's Word is as relevant today as it was thousands of years ago and its power will not be diminished in the millennia to come because it is the operating manual authored by the manufacturer of the universe. However, it is the antiquated and anachronistic way the Bible is taught to this generation of children that is obscuring its value as way too many young people choose to trade in their religion for the world's approval.

The first clue we may be heading in the wrong direction is that the Bible continues to be taught as it has been for centuries. It is as if we are allowing our ancestors from medieval times or pilgrim days to teach our kids instead of doing it ourselves. Imagine that someone from the time of King James or Benjamin Franklin came to your church to try to inspire young people about God. That person's clothes would not be the only outdated articles. Church leaders in the time of the Roman Empire, the Dark Ages, and the Crusades were not effective couriers of those teachings at all. Wars, killings, and conflict defined their worldview of the intended message of peace and love from the man who was killed by a similar mob.

The second clue that our interpretation of the Bible needs to be adjusted is that many of the things we teach forces teenagers and college students to choose between their science books and their Bible. Although science provides a treasure trove of information that could be used to reinforce faith, our interpretation of Scripture drives a wedge between the two.

We are basically teaching the same things our ancestors taught, just with a different backdrop and downbeat even though the metaphors and word pictures used by authors of scripture may have long since expired. For example, the apostle Paul painted a word picture about a soldier's weaponry for the church in Ephesus to inspire them to utilize God's power in their lives. Correlating God's Word to the "sword of the Spirit" (Eph. 6:17 NIV) would have created powerful emotions for those people in the first century. However, for any kid growing up in today's world playing video games or seeing combat movies demonstrating modern weaponry, the *sword* metaphor is now irrelevant. After all, politicians in Washington aren't debating *sword control* legislation or incorporating swords into military armament. Anyone who remembers the scene in the movie *Raiders of the Lost Ark* where an assassin confronts Indiana Jones with a menacing sword but then Jones matter-of-factly pulls out a pistol and shoots him, is well aware of how obsolete swords and other first century word pictures can be in today's Bible classes. The lesson Paul was teaching about preparation and conviction will be relevant until the end of time. However, each generation must sync Paul's metaphors with word pictures of their own to ensure the intended emotional connection is made.

Just like the class exercise where the teacher whispers something to the first child in the class and it comes out as something altogether different by the time it gets to the last child, the teachings from the man from Galilee are barely recognizable today after being filtered by the religious winds of the past two thousand years. A lot has happened since preachers were spewing fire and brimstone from the pulpit hundreds of years ago. In centuries past, very few people were educated, and since ignorance breeds fear and superstition, preachers and teachers were able to control their congregations by playing on those fears. In a way, it was like scriptural abuse, where ignorance allowed preachers to psychologically beat up people about how unworthy they were and how scared they should be of God. In fairness to them, they taught the Bible in this way because that was how it was taught to them. It was like the blind leading the blind.

It reminds me of the scene in the movie 7 where the wizard was able to scare Doroth, nearly to death with loud noises and threats of doom. Ultimately, Dorothy's dog, Toto, pulled the curtain back to reveal the wizard's identity and expose his humanity and ineptness. For this generation, where is Toto when you need him? Witches in Salem had to pay the price of ignorance with their lives while for centuries wicked men dressed in religious attire persecuted anyone who didn't follow their instructions.

Every generation since Jesus walked on this earth has been sitting on a spiritual goldmine without knowing where it was or how to get it. If we were holding a winning lottery ticket, our emotions could not be restrained. What we possess is of far greater value than any winning lottery ticket without even considering heaven, so those emotions should be even greater for this journey. As in Dorothy's hunt for home, the treasure of God can only be found when it dawns on us what we are really looking for. That is the first step in finding it.

CHAPTER 2

The Treasure of God

It has now been twenty-six years since a safe said to belong to Al Capone was opened on a live television broadcast. Much of the nation was glued to their television sets to see what kind of treasure might be unlocked as the safe was opened, revealing the secrets that had been hidden for decades. To the dismay and amusement of the millions of people watching, the safe contained nothing of real value, making people feel gullible and cynical about their belief that something valuable might have been in the safe.

As teenagers go off to college untethered from the religion of their parents and grandparents, they will make life choices based on whatever creates the most value in their lives. The decision whether to include religion in that pursuit or not is directly related to what they think the treasure of God is worth or whether they think it actually exists. It is time to crack open the Lord's safe and show them the treasure of God before the church loses any more young people. To help identify where the treasure of God is, let's begin with a story.

The Magic Coat

You just had a very difficult day at work, and nothing else in your life seems to be going well either. Friends seem distant, coworkers are growling at you, and even things at church are a distraction. You go to church every service and teach class whenever possible, but there just seems to be something missing at church and in life. Sometimes it feels like religious people are some of the unhappiest people on earth. You don't feel good about yourself, and everything seems to be imploding around you. So you decide to go for a walk in the woods just to sort things out. Off in the distance, you happen to see a small cave. To feed your curiosity, you decide to take a look inside.

Upon entering the cave, you see a gift-wrapped package sitting on a ledge. As you wonder who might have lost this package, you look for a card to see whose it is so you can return it to him or her. However, there is no card or means of identifying whose it is, so you decide to open it and look inside. To your surprise, there is a coat inside the box that appears to be your size. Since it won't hurt anything, you try it on, and it fits perfectly, as if it were made just for you. While you marvel at what you have found, something starts happening within you that lets you know this is not an ordinary coat. It is a magic coat. You can't describe it, but you are a completely changed person. You emerge from the cave with the coat on, and although you don't look any different than you did when you entered the cave, that coat has started affecting your life.

It doesn't take long for people to notice the changes. You have incredible skills and qualities that would make any Bible character proud and some even jealous. It is obvious there is a flood of power unlike anything you have ever experienced flowing through you. You have joy that eclipses anything ever seen so you get up every day ready to take on the world. Your compassion for others has no peer in that you can see joy and pain in people by simply reading their faces, and your ability to love now has no boundaries. The self-esteem issues that previously plagued your life have long since evaporated.

Although this is just a story, isn't this the life we all want? Well, maybe we need to stop and actually ask ourselves that question. What kind of life do we want? Whether it pertains to friends, family, career, or just being a couch potato letting the world go by, there is a specific price for whatever kind of life we want to have which will, by definition, influence the kind of life our heirs will have available to them as well. Whether we realize it or not, we are in the process of helping to raise our great-, great-, great-, great-grandchildren who we will never meet. Each choice we make will have consequences for our families for generations, good or bad. So let's ask that question again: what kind of life do we want to have and how much are we willing to pay to have it? Are we happy with the life we currently have? If not, what changes need to be made to correct its trajectory?

None of us start out with boundaries; essentially, our boundaries are self-inflicted, although sometimes they are from someone else's expectations of the life they thought we should have. Obstacles toward the magic coat life can come from so many directions. There are hundreds of stories in the Bible where people had to overcome stumbling blocks in their race of life in order to cross the finish line in faith. That is the one common characteristic of those listed in the book of Hebrews' hall of fame: they all died in faith. Although they may have encountered numerous distractions in running toward God and perhaps even failed along the way, each of them finished the race in faith. There is a reason for every word in the Bible; the reason that the stories of these heroes were mentioned was to show what is possible in our lives, not to rub our noses in their accomplishments.

The most important thing to understand about faith in God and His Son is this: it is possible for each of us to be greater than all of the servants of God mentioned in the Bible, combined. God has placed no restrictions on how much of His nature we can biologically cram into our minds. The only boundaries involve our humanity where those characteristics are stored and protected. When we understand the only boundaries that exist in our lives are the ones we erect, it is even more insane to entangle ourselves in counterproductive things, which will be covered in greater detail a little later. Because people are leaving the church, it must mean they cannot fathom what it would be like to have all of the traits the magic coat makes possible. If they could, they certainly would not be heading for the doors as they do now.

Who would not want to be like Superman? Imagine what it would be like to be a superhero and not just wear their pajamas. Imagine being able to fly around and be so strong that you could help everyone and stop evil in its tracks. As you know, superheroes have their own special set of skills that we would love to possess. At the same time, each of them has a specific weakness that can destroy them. Such is the life of a superhero as well as the people who want to be like them.

Now imagine that the special qualities of every superhero known to man (and comic books) are combined and bestowed on one single person on earth to be used for the good of mankind. Whatever happened in that person's life prior to this infusion of spirit is a distant memory as power now flows throughout that person's body and soul. Guilt and doubt have been replaced with a dynamic life focused on helping others. That person could be any one of us and every one of us in the context of a powerful spiritual life.

Young people leave the church because they don't see Superman; they just see the Kryptonite and the damage it does. The reality is that each of us can be that person in more ways than we can count; we can have the ability to affect more lives than any superhero ever could. The thing that gets lost in our teachings is that each of us can have those qualities in abundance, even more than is described in the Bible.

We can be wiser than Solomon, stronger and more cunning than David, more diplomatic than Barnabas, a better leader than Moses, have more faith than Abraham, be more patient than Joseph or Job, and be more effective than Paul, all at the same time. Do we understand exactly what that means? These are some of the greatest servants of God who ever lived, but their contributions would pale by comparison if we would just get out of our own way and hand God the remote. We are not limited in the number of God's attributes we have or their magnitude. Where in the world did we get the idea that God's power is somehow limited to a few gifts? Young people would not be running away from the church if they saw it as a training ground for unlimited ability.

The urgency of this pursuit is that we don't know when these gifts might be needed for extraordinary events. For example, if we knew that ten years from now our children would perish in a fire because we weren't strong enough to carry them out, we would spend every day for the next ten years in strength training to be able to save them. That analogy could also pertain to generations from now.

Just like a first-aid kit that has numerous things in it that may never be needed, we don't know which of these gifts will be needed as arrows in our quiver. If we knew which spiritual gifts would be needed in our lives, we could just focus on acquiring those, freeing up the rest of our time to do what we wanted to do. Unfortunately, life is not scripted that way. Therefore, we need to take all of the gifts mentioned in the Bible and make them our own—all of them. This pursuit should be done with such passion and emotion that everyone who sees us knows the source of this incredible power. Everyone who believes in God needs to become fully aware of the miraculous life that is possible by finding the treasure. That pursuit should also manifest itself in power during our time together as believers.

Snowball Effect
Now for the location of the treasure: the treasure of God that has been so elusive in its acquisition for God's people through the ages is simply Jehovah God Himself. It is not the personification of God that is necessary to teach young minds about God. It is not a caricature of God that barely resembles His nature. He is not someone to be feared but an awesome spiritual power to plug into and become as radiant as our faith will allow. The treasure is God Almighty in all His glory and power. That is the life that is available to all who believe, pressed down and running over. It is a life where every single characteristic of God can be infused into our lives, giving us the ability to affect the world in extraordinary ways.

Imagine that every person trying to follow Jesus' teachings

developed those traits to the max. What an incredible synergy that would create! God's power would overwhelm the world, like a snowball rolling downhill. Child abuse would be eradicated, and domestic violence would be wiped from the earth. There would not be a single child ever starve to death again, and all parents would train their children in the nurture and admonition of the Lord—not because the Bible said to but because they could see its inordinate value for themselves. Divorce would be a foreign concept for followers of Christ, and crosses would no longer have to be erected on the side of the road in memory of loved ones lost.

Unfortunately, child abuse and domestic violence are still global scourges, even in the church. Young children around the world go without food while the lives of intoxicated teenagers and young adults are remembered in roadside memorials. The divorce rate in the church is similar to the rest of the world while the Internet controls the minds and money of churchgoers almost as much as those who are not.

This will continue until the church wakes up and starts teaching the Bible the way it was intended so people can visualize the extraordinary power that is available to them. As it is, there is an enormous chasm separating legacy religion from people searching for spiritual relevance. This chasm exists because older Christians were never allowed to question their religion. It became a catatonic exercise of repetition, but this generation of young people needs to see more evidence than ever before to believe unbelievable things. It is not about one group compromising with the other so they reach some consensus of tolerance. It is about combining spiritual assets to make God's power and light more visible.

Let's illustrate how the snowball effect is supposed to work. There are a lot of famous individuals in our culture who people would like to emulate. Let's use an example like Taylor Swift, a famous country and pop singer and entertainer who is liked by girls of all ages to illustrate this potential domino effect. At each of Taylor's concerts, there are hundreds of young girls holding up signs stating what they think of her and how much they want to be like her. Because she seems intent on helping young girls with their self-esteem so they will like themselves as they are, let's imagine that each of these girls got her wish. Imagine that thousands of girls at these concerts bought into that thought and were inspired to shed their self-esteem issues and do whatever was best for their lives instead of following a self-destructive culture. Imagine each of them doing what was in her best interest instead of feeling she had to do things so others would like her. There would then be no need for girls to have sex so boys would like them. Rather, they would begin controlling their own destiny and not engage in stupid behavior. This would empower young girls and help them embrace being a daughter of the King.

Because each subsequent generation could see how much better life is when enveloped with love for oneself and others, within just a few generations, this number would expand to tens of millions of girls not enslaved by low self-esteem. That is just arithmetic. By definition, this would force the boys around them to become the men they were intended to be. That is just hormones. That would eventually translate into every husband treating his wife as she should be treated and vice versa. It would mean parents would raise their children in a way that would encourage them to be all they could be because the massive value of doing that would be obvious.

In less than one hundred years of this snowball effect of young girls seeing how to have a better life, it would envelop the world like kudzu where each generation passes on to the next this better life. This is just an illustration of how quickly something as simple as self-esteem could snowball in such a short time. The effect could be much more pronounced with the full power of God. The fact that so many people in Christianity struggle with self-esteem issues, especially young ladies, means we may not have painted the picture of God correctly. Girls who were force fed the tenets of a religion where women were supposed to be submissive to men were already starting behind the eight ball.

Now imagine the sheer math of this snowball, not just for one hundred years but for two thousand years. This is how Christianity was supposed to be sold or rather how it would have sold itself if each generation had let its light shine.

If the things the man from Galilee taught had penetrated each generation, the last wife to get beaten by her husband would have happened centuries ago. The last child to die from starvation would have been buried long before Columbus sailed the ocean blue, and all children would be raised without the turmoil that stupidity and ignorance create. The snowball effect would have magnified the power of God for each subsequent generation so they would have living examples of how it was supposed to be implemented.

This will not happen just because we want it to. We can't just wave a magic wand or say a few prayers and then all of a sudden become this gift-bearing servant of God that can change the world. Is anything of great value ever easily found? As every exceptional athlete or musician knows, accomplishing great things takes extraordinary effort and focus, and learning to walk in God's shoes is no different. By focusing every ounce of our mental and spiritual strength toward tapping into God's power while eliminating distractions, anyone can become the beacon of light that changes the world. If young people could visualize the church as this incredible, life-invigorating river of hope and experience it themselves, we would be planning parking lot expansions rather than trying to figure out why believers have quit coming.

It will take help from all believers to resurrect the faith of young people lost in the forest of disbelief. Therefore, you are invited on a Scripture safari into this jungle of faith and doubt to help them navigate their way to the treasure of God. In essence, we are going on a treasure hunt through the Bible, seeking spiritual gold so enormous it could sustain all generations to come as well as the faith of those teenagers currently being poisoned by the arrows of opposition they were never trained to deflect.

On this journey, we will encounter numerous forks in the road, paths to choose which will determine the success or failure of our mission. As we study the Bible on this expedition, there will be many things to consider and decisions to make that we never had to think about when these kids were growing up, or at least we didn't think we had to make. Now we have no choice but to share the things we believe and why we believe them since their faith may be riding on our answers.

Our inclination is to make a mad dash into the jungle of faith and doubt, grab them by the ear and march them right out and back into the church building. However, that is how we got into this mess in the first place. We are about to find out that perhaps, we have been the problem all along. After all, faith cannot be forced on anyone. These young people are going to decide for themselves whether the religious diet we have been feeding them since they were in diapers can sustain them in the world they now live.

Let me suggest that instead of treating faith as a commodity to be rescued on this treasure hunt, the expedition itself should become part of our spiritual DNA. Instead of rushing through the jungle to find faith and then trying to inoculate it against everything attacking it, we should embrace doubt as a component of a strong faith. As can be seen in the lives of most Bible characters like David, Moses, Elijah, Peter, and Paul, faith typically grows by going two steps forward and one step backward so that a strong foundation is laid. Until faith becomes knowledge when our humanity is detached from our minds, overcoming doubts will be the catalyst for building a strong faith.

There is a point in the lives of children where parents and adults should quit talking down to them about God and what they are to believe. Instead, parents should enjoy a leisurely stroll into this jungle with their children and address everything in the Bible that doesn't make sense rather than blow these things off as something not meant to be known. We don't have to be Bible scholars to help our children figure out what to believe and what not to believe; we just have to be their parents, helping them navigate successfully through the maze of information that creates and destroys faith.

On this journey, when you come to each fork in the road, imagine a college student standing there, having lost her faith, not knowing what to believe anymore. Before proceeding, be sure to explain why you believe what you believe about each choice you have made and then consider whether anyone that age could understand your point of view. Even though your children may be way too young for this journey right now, one day they could be that college student, struggling to believe. The stakes are high because the faith of our children are riding on it; be sure to choose the path they can believe that leads to a successful life filled with God's power.

CHAPTER 3

For Heaven's Sake

How would you describe heaven? No really, how would you describe heaven? What are its coordinates? Is it really up "there"? Is God seated on an actual throne in heaven? If it is so important to Christians, why can't anyone explain it in a way that biologically or metaphysically makes sense? In the history of mankind, nobody has actually ever described heaven as it really is. Certainly, it is described by preachers and teachers related to what it is like, but it has never been described by its actual composition or coordinates. If it had, then many of the church's teachings about things tied to heaven would not hold water. Hold that thought for a moment.

Everyone I know likes dessert. There may be times when our eyes are bigger than our stomachs so there isn't room for dessert after a big meal. However, if we were given the choice between green beans and chocolate cake, it is unlikely the green beans would ever leave the bowl.

When I was growing up, it was always a special treat when my grandmother, who lived in another state, paid our family a visit. During each visit, she would take us to a local restaurant known for their hot fudge cakes and sundaes, and after we cleaned our plates, she would let us indulge ourselves. It was during one of those dinners that we started a new tradition that has lasted a lifetime. After ordering dinner and while waiting for our meals to arrive, my brother and I would wonder out loud why we couldn't have our dessert first. After all, why should we have to wait for something so good? There certainly was no question whether hot fudge cake hors d'oeuvres would ruin the appetites of growing teenage boys. After puzzled looks from our parents, our grandmother called the waiter over to have him bring two hot fudge sundaes before bringing the rest of the meal. Ever since, whenever practical, I consume my dessert before anything else. Although I may not eat as much food as I did as a teenager, my choice of appetizer still comes from the dessert menu.

The way Christianity currently teaches its members about heaven makes it seem a lot like dessert. In just about every Sunday school and worship service in the church, heaven is described as a place we go after we have finished our time on earth. In that regard, if life is the main course, then heaven is something to be enjoyed afterward, like dessert as a reward for good behavior. Actually, it is even better than that, but in the church we have been taught we can't have dessert until the meal is over. It has been ingrained in us that if we follow the rules and clean our plates, then heaven awaits. Scripture conjures up mental images of a courtroom where God is the judge sitting on a throne who will open the books about us and then decide if we get dessert. Although there will be no actual throne or books, the intended purpose of this word picture was to help believers maintain their focus on the difficult path in front of them in the first century.

Every teacher knows that a metaphor has a shelf life directly related to its intended audience. Throughout time, unknown places and things have been fertile grounds for the teaching and training of neophytes of any discipline. That is because inspiration is unlimited when placed in unknown environs. The North Pole was an effective location for Santa Claus in the nineteenth century, and the sky worked well as the location for heaven until the last one hundred years or so. When the Wright brothers led the assault on the unknown reaches of the sky, it should have prompted godly people to transport heaven from its metaphoric physical location described in Scripture to its actual ethereal residence. The metaphor of heaven being somewhere up in the sky allowed the eight or nine men who penned the New Testament to effectively teach and inspire their audience. However, continuing to do so today robs heaven of its power by limiting its reality.

In the Old Testament, heaven was not even mentioned as a goal or destination. People were described at their death as having "gone the way of all the earth" (1 Kings 2:2 ESV) with no mention of heaven. Their goal was to please God so life would go well for them and the rest would take care of itself. In our lives, God's Word should be so powerful that, had heaven never been mentioned, nothing about our lives would change. In that regard, heaven could have just been a great surprise, making it like a delicious dessert.

It may be difficult to grasp based on our current teachings, but heaven is not a place we go when we die. Heaven is where we live when God lives in us because God and heaven are inseparable. After all, God didn't leave Heaven to reside in us. God is everywhere, so heaven is everywhere. Heaven is not a physical place in that it has no coordinates; rather, place that encompasses God's nature. Actually, th *place* is an oxymoron because spiritual entitie peace, and patience are real and essential compone... lives, though void of coordinates. Heaven should be the same. Our faith in God affords us all the rights, privileges, power, discipline, sacrifice, love, and commitment that membership in this spiritual community provides.

As such, heaven is not a goal or destination but is an integral part of the journey of life because that is what faith in God creates. After all, Paul says that our citizenship "is" in heaven (Phil. 3:20 NIV), not "will be" in heaven. It is a lot easier to understand this by thinking of dessert as part of the meal rather than something that happens after the meal is over. Incorporating heaven into our daily walk is like eating our dessert first and then savoring each subsequent moment.

The relevance of this is that by teaching heaven as a place you go when you die, even though teenagers might not die for eighty years or so, it is impossible for them to see value where none is required. After all, if death is not perceived to be potentially imminent, as it was in the first century, and nobody has ever explained the advantages of faith, then what is the urgency about emulating God? The judgment metaphor may have been appropriate for an audience with a life expectancy of less than fifty years, but people today need to understand how God intertwined in their lives can produce better results than flailing away on their own.

Certainly, this is different than the church's teachings on the subject, although the church cannot explain some of its teachings that were developed centuries ago, when held up to e light of scrutiny. Heaven is eternal, but so is our spirit as well as the mind where it resides. To make sense of this, let's go outside in the middle of the day and try to see the stars in the sky. Obviously, we can't because the sun's light dominates our view. Even at night, clouds can obscure our sight. Although nobody would question whether stars are always up in the sky, they can only be seen absent these distractions.

To better understand heaven, give this a try: sit in a dark room by yourself, taking only your thoughts with you. Without all of life's distractions, see if you are able to focus on heavenly things that are typically unseen while juggling life's trials and temptations. In that quiet room if we focus, we can almost smell the cookies our grandmother baked or see our grandfather working on his farm. In spirit, we can take our minds anywhere we want to, using our memories to navigate between any chosen person or event. Without even blinking an eye, we can go sit on our favorite beach and almost hear the ocean waves. This is all done in spirit. There are no limits to the things our spiritual minds can encounter about heaven if we reorient our lives to allow it. It is only when the dog starts barking or the phone starts ringing that our view of heaven evaporates like the stars in the sky as the sun comes up. When we are still, and God lives in us through faith, heaven becomes a part of us. When we take our last breath the distractions will end, making our view of God in heaven permanent.

So now you've come to a fork in the road about heaven. What do you really believe and can you explain it? What does it mean that God lives in us? How would you explain it to our college student struggling to believe so that it makes sense? Our young people are being bombarded with dozens of things

for which we never prepared them. If we cannot ar
questions for them, then who can?

There are numerous paths ahead which must b_ ..._ _
to guide our kids safely to the treasure. Some of the questions
they will face are related to God, the Rapture, Jesus' return,
interpreting the Bible, baptism, Satan, the worship service,
women's roles, men's roles and the church itself. In the end, we
need to empower teenagers and young adults to defend their
faith by showing them how to use the Bible effectively in this
Internet age.

There is a simple yet timeless method for unraveling the
Bible's clues about any subject. This method of understanding
the Bible will be relevant until the last star is found in the
universe, probably millions of years from now. There is nothing
that would glorify God more than for His creatures at the
top of the food chain to take the words addressed to spiritual
neophytes in the Bible and sustain mankind for that length of
time. The way to interpret Scripture so that it will always be
relevant is by looking at it in its proper context.

Anyone evaluating what they really believe about heaven will
certainly recall John's account of Jesus words in his gospel. These
words are recorded in the fourteenth chapter of John as Jesus
related a story about heaven to his disciples. To encourage and
comfort them about their impending spiritual warfare, Jesus
told his disciples this story while they were in the Upper Room.
He would have had ample time later after his resurrection to
share this information but it would have a more powerful effect
on them by sharing those words right before they deserted their
General. After all, their hearts were troubled (John 14:1), so
in their time of anxiety, He told them something intended to

accomplish that purpose. In His words of encouragement, as soon as we hear the words "in my father's house" (John 14:2), today we immediately know it is a metaphor because a spiritual God doesn't live in a physical house. There is no physical house and it has no physical rooms nor walls. If you do believe that God does reside in a house with rooms and that this is not just an encouraging word picture, you need to be able to explain all of the details of that belief. When Jesus said that when He came back He would take them to be with Him (John 14:3), it is all either metaphoric or they are still in some holding tank waiting for Jesus to return. Which one are you going to try to explain to our college student?

Although the words of the Bible were not written to us, they can have powerful meaning for us, as long as we filter them through the intended audience first. Just like them, we can be encouraged and strengthened by the words of these inspired writers so that the power of God can flow through us.

We can have a life that is defined by every attribute of God. If people thought that life could be derived by sitting in a church pew, they would be standing in line, waiting for the church doors to open. However, we know that is not the case. The goal of the church must be to illustrate the teachings of Jesus in a way that makes people want to become part of the group by demonstrating that value. After all, nobody wants a tasteless dessert, for heaven's sake.

CHAPTER 4

Resurrecting Faith

There is a fine line that separates faith from gullibility and religion from superstition.

While walking down the street you notice a bag setting on the side of the road. Your curiosity gets the better of you so you open the bag to see what is inside and you can't believe what you have found. Although you don't understand everything you are reading, it is obvious to you that this bag contains the cures for every type of cancer on earth. Brain cancer and breast cancer; lung cancer and colon cancer; throat and liver cancer- inside this bag are the cures for every cancer known to man. The magnitude of what you have stumbled upon begins to hit you like a ton of bricks as it dawns on you that this could change the world and even alter the course of history. People destined to die leaving small children behind would now be able to live and raise them because of your discovery. People would no longer have to live in fear of cancer because it is about to be wiped off the face of the earth. It has to be shared as quickly as possible so that it can change lives. What a blessing this will be!

But wait a minute; what if nobody believes you. What if every doctor presented with this information ridicules you for thinking you actually found something so valuable. What if you go share this with everyone you come in contact with and they all just laugh at you for being so gullible to believe something so preposterous. You think to yourself: "well, after all, it was just in a bag on the side of the road". So you toss the bag back on the ground and go on your way relieved that your good judgment saved you so much embarrassment. The bag may have the cure for cancer but without faith that it does, it is just another bag on the side of the road. There is, indeed, a fine line that separates faith from gullibility, and religion from superstition.

There is nothing more powerful on earth than faith. Faith is more powerful than all of the nuclear power plants and weaponry combined, even in the heart and mind of a single child. Faith can indeed move mountains. Faith can provide the motivation for people to follow their dreams and change the world, even altering the course of history. Faith can empower a woman to lift a car that has trapped her child because of the focused passion driving that faith. It can also give a young shepherd boy the speed, cunning, and focus to kill an experienced warrior nearly ten feet tall by following the path faith creates. Although logic erects boundaries intended to protect us, faith has no such boundaries, making impossible things possible.

Although faith has such incredible value, it cannot be bought or sold, and it has no price. It is not something that can be traded like baseball cards. It can't be stored or inventoried, nor can it be socked away for a rainy day. It cannot be taught in school so that at the end of the course, a person will have acquired faith. In fact, it can never be acquired; it can only be created. Faith has a voracious appetite, and if it is not constantly fed evidence, it will eventually die even while sitting in a church pew. The most important thing to understand about faith is what creates it as well as what destroys it.

Faith is not a religious thing or a theological thing. Faith is purely biological in that faith is manufactured solely in the mind. While knowledge occupies certain cells in one area of the brain, faith is generated in other parts of the brain, especially related to a person's spirit and emotions. In effect, evidence activates the launch codes of faith, whether that pertains to believing the things the Bible teaches are true or whether we believe our favorite football team can come back from a thirty-point deficit. A child whose mom has picked them up after basketball practice at exactly 4:30 the whole season begins to get her things together at 4:29 because she has reason to believe her mom is about to arrive based on the evidence her mind has to process. Another child whose mom has been late for pick up the whole season doesn't even flinch at 4:30 because of the same reasoning. It's all in the mind and how the mind processes its inputs. Basically, it is all about evidence or the lack thereof.

Developing a Childlike Faith

From the time children are born until they are adults, we make it extremely hard for them to know what things they are supposed to believe along the way. In the first third of their pre-adult lives, they are supposed to believe there are two men who can see them when they are sleeping and know when they are awake. Both men supposedly know when they have been bad or good and will give good things to the children who have been good. We tell our children one of them lives at the North Pole and delivers gifts to all the good little boys and girls around the world on a certain night of the year. He also wears a red suit with black boots and a white beard, and after Thanksgiving, they can actually see him at a shopping mall. We also tell them that the other man up in the sky is somewhere watching everything they do, and if they are good, they will also get good things from Him. However, there is no mall to go see God and sit on His lap.

Children at that age would never think to ask how Santa Claus could possibly visit every child in the world in one night. Neither could they possibly conceive how the other man— God—can watch everybody on earth at the same time. It's a good thing that children that age cannot think to ask those types of questions because their parents wouldn't be able to answer them without making something up. Children are incredibly trusting of what parents tell them at this very young age. Because their parents have been there all of their lives taking care of their needs, they will believe anything they are told by the people who love them most. They are going to blindly believe in Santa Claus, and they are going to blindly believe in God simply because their parents told them what to believe.

Eventually, the Santa bubble bursts. Whether it is some kid on the playground making fun of them for believing in Santa or their older brother doing the same, eventually all children realize the obvious: the North Pole is just a very cold place. By the time they learn the truth about the jolly old man, they will also be old enough to comprehend the spiritual aspects of the Christmas season. Transitioning from a personified version of giving, compassion, and gratitude to its spiritual complement is possible because of the development of a child's mind over time.

It is only about ten years from the time they l
Santa Claus until they go off to college and less tim
before they have a set of car keys in their hands, g
a measure of freedom. In that time, they may be dragged to church every time the doors are open or go to church camp every year or even have mountaintop experiences on a regular basis. None of that may have any bearing on whether their faith in the other man from their childhood survives the spiritual assault of adulthood.

The irony is that we do a great job of transitioning a child from Santa Claus to the spirit of Christmas while doing virtually nothing about the same transition from a personified God to the real, spiritual God. It would be ludicrous to think you could teach a fifteen-year-old boy or girl that Santa Claus is real. However, we teach God the same way to a five-year-old as we do to a twenty-five-year-old. God is real; the personified version of God is not. It should be irrational to think that someone could go to church for fifty years or more and still think the personified description of God is anything near His true nature. Doing so only makes God seem to be some type of cartoon character. God personified is a great teaching tool for understanding God, just as Santa Claus is a great teaching tool for children during the holiday season. However, there comes a time to put away childish things.

Teaching a personified God to ages capable of understanding God as spirit will stunt their spiritual growth, and it could even kill their faith. Growing in the knowledge of God for any age requires evidence of God. Unless they are given evidence of the things we want them to believe, their faith in God will go the way of their faith in Santa Claus once they are teenagers.

The church's reaction to this paradigm is bewildering. It is as if we are scared of the inordinate examination the Internet creates for the things we believe. Cults are afraid of scrutiny; the church should not be. Instead of sticking our heads back in our shells to hide from the scrutiny, we should embrace it. The Bible is constructed to withstand the wind of even this generation's scrutiny of its teachings—just not in the way we currently teach it. The way to stop the erosion of faith in the church is to fight fire with fire by hitting teenagers in the church with everything they will face on the college campus and letting the chips fall where they may. If we want our young people to possess the treasure and utilize its full worth in their lives, then we will have to show them its location first. *[handwritten: WHY THE LOCATION, WHY IS THAT NECESSARY]*

The most effective way to teach the Bible to children is to *[handwritten: AS MENTIONED EARLIER "THE COORDINATES OF HEAVEN"]* continue sharing stories about God to children ten years of age and younger through personification. Once they are old enough for driver training, they are also old enough for spiritual training toward their college years. At that point, they need to prepare for the spiritual assault they will face all too soon from their teachers explaining the difference between God as He is rather than the personified God He is not. Teenagers will likely begin to question just about everything they have been taught around this age, so this is an ideal time to guide their thought process toward a better understanding of God. Children between the ages of ten and fifteen should have the Bible presented as a transition from one to the other based on their individual maturity, knowledge, and curiosity level.

Blowing apart the personification of God to older teenagers by unleashing His full nature and power will help them prepare for college because there are no limits to the things that might be

[handwritten: WHAT DOES THAT MEAN. BAPG!]

initiated there. The goal is to show them evidence o
also helping them train their minds to weed out no
type of analysis will actually show that God is mc
than anyone has dared to imagine and that the ricl
to His people are also greater than they can possibly dream
about. Of course, it may also dismantle parts of the religion
of Christianity that should have been discarded centuries ago
anyway. The way Christianity was launched in the first century
was supposed to be the booster rocket to take it to its intended
orbit. However, it remained chained to the ground because of the
religion it quickly became. Hence, the first generation to make a
sustained attack on its teachings would expose the weaknesses
of the things being taught. This is that generation.

I once watched a video about a golf shot Phil Mickelson was
about to perform. Mickelson is an incredible golfer who has won
four major tournaments, as well as dozens of other ones. He is
also known for being able to pull off incredible shots. In this
video, he was going to try to hit a flop shot with a lofted wedge by
immediately elevating the ball as quickly as possible. The thing
that made the shot memorable, and why it was videotaped in the
first place, was that Mickelson's coach was standing right in front
of him, only about four feet away. Mickelson would take a full
swing at the ball, and if he misjudged it at all, it would strike the
coach at full force. To nobody's surprise, Mickelson successfully
made the shot. Both of these men had faith the shot would be
made but for different reasons, even though the consequences for
one would have been more severe than the other. Mickelson had
great faith because he had executed that shot numerous times,
and his coach had faith because he had seen evidence of that skill
set. Evidence has a powerful effect on our capacity to believe.

CHAPTER 5

License to Teach

Almost forty years ago I received my pilot's license. From beginning to end, the whole process took eight weeks and to do it in this timeframe, I flew just about every day. In addition to the flight training required, knowledge about navigation and communication with air traffic control was also required along with learning the airplane's equipment and rules of flight. After passing the written exam and completing the required flight training, I was ready for my check ride with an FAA flight examiner.

The examination process was fairly simple although it was very intense. When the check ride was over, the examiner completed the paperwork necessary for my license. I will always remember the words he told me before giving the license to me that have served me well in flight and in other areas of my life. He told me what I earned from my flight training and examination was not a license to fly; rather, it was only a license to learn how to fly. He was basically telling me that anyone can learn how to manipulate the controls of an airplane, but it takes a lifetime to learn how to be a pilot and, as such, that training never ends.

Regardless of the discipline, knowledge is an important component. Whether it involves sports, music, karate, yoga, dance, or any number of other disciplines, what we know about the principles of that discipline helps to facilitate broadening the dimensions of its use. The same applies to studying the Bible. We can know everything there is to know about the Bible, but unless that knowledge leads to an application of it in our lives, then that effort is in vain. In effect, faith just gives us a license to learn about God the way the inspired writers intended, which helps us navigate toward the treasure.

Lesson Plan

Imagine that Albert Einstein has been commissioned to teach a group of thirty first-graders the complexities of quantum physics. It would be hard enough for anyone to teach kids this age to play nice on the playground, but that is the project. To add to this difficulty, Mr. Einstein will not be allowed to teach them himself. He can only pull one child from the class and teach him or her how to teach the rest of the class all the nuances of quantum physics. And if that isn't impossible enough, the use of any pictures, diagrams, videos, chalkboards, or computers is forbidden.

Einstein would have to try to demonstrate everything that a six-year-old could grasp simply by the words coming out of his mouth at a level of information the child could understand while accomplishing the ultimate goal. Every word this child tells the class will be recorded and then used as the gold standard for teaching subsequent generations about quantum physics.

You would be correct to note how silly it would be to think that any child could possibly grasp the subject matter at that level of information. It is even more ridiculous to think he or she could then teach his or her class something so complex, much less use his or her words to teach future generations. However, that is exactly what we have done to Moses and all of the other authors of Scripture.

Let's look at it another way. Your second-grade teacher may have had her bachelor's degree, her master's degree, and even her doctorate in given areas of education. However, the things she would teach her seven-year-olds about math and science would obviously be based on her class's capacity to absorb information rather than her level of knowledge. She might be a whiz at calculus and astronomy, but all she would be able to teach second graders would be simple arithmetic and a few facts about the planets in our solar system. In addition, in order for everyone in the class to grasp the intended material, she would have to teach in a way that everyone in the class could understand and not just the top students. The mistake the church makes in its interpretation of Scripture is trying to discern the authors' intent viewed through the prism of our knowledge and understanding after centuries of consideration and perspective, instead of allowing those writers to teach their intended audience through theirs. The Bible was written at the level of the audience, not the level of the author.

Coaching to Win

I had never been to a church camp while growing up, so when the opportunity presented itself to become a counselor after my junior year in high school, I jumped at the chance. The new interstate was going through the old camp our church owned, so that meant that a new one would have to be built somewhere else. The first year it opened would be that opportunity. Because it was my first year to ever lay eyes on a church camp, I was very excited about getting the first of that two-week commitment under way.

As part of the field activities each week, they would divide the campers into different teams for each event. Since these were third and fourth graders, it wasn't a big deal to put girls and boys on the same team and then play a round robin tournament for each event. Since I would be going to college on a baseball scholarship the next year, the event I enjoyed the most was softball.

The rules for the softball competition at this level were simple: it would be two pitch, coach pitch, with the coach being able to play the field for his own team. That meant that the counselor would pitch the ball to his own team, and each batter had to get one of only two possible pitches in play or they would be out. In addition, the counselor would play the field to help his own group of players. As you can imagine, the athletic talent level for this coed group of kids from all walks of life was varied. Some had played some ball before, and some had not. During the first week of camp with teams evenly divided, my team won all five games, and on Friday night's closing ceremony, they all received their ribbons for being champions of the softball field.

The person who divided all of the campers into their teams each week was the camp's assistant director. He was a well-known football coach everyone loved, and he was a good friend. As my team went up to get their softball ribbons on that first Friday night, the assistant director whispered to me that I had done a good job with these kids. Being full of myself, I thanked him and then braggingly told him that it didn't matter who he put on my team the next week, we would win the ribbons again.

He just smiled back at me, and when the next week's camp started Sunday night, I found out why.

Like any good coach, he loved competition, and I guess I had foolishly thrown down the gauntlet. When the softball team sheets were handed out, I looked at how the teams had been divided. I saw that I had been given the kids who had never played any type of sport in their lives. They were the smartest kids in the camp, but they were also the least likely to ever receive an athletic award. And since I had all of the non-athletes on my team, the other teams were therefore stacked with the best athletes. I was sure that Coach was smiling to himself somewhere.

Since there was no available practice time, I gathered my team together and gave them some simple instructions. I told them if they would listen to me and do everything I asked, on Friday night they would receive ribbons for their effort. I assured them they would be able to walk past all of those good athletes at the awards ceremony and receive their ribbons while their parents took their pictures.

Having no time to teach them about softball, I simply told them how to hold a bat and exactly where to swing it. I assured them that the ball would be exactly there when their bat came around. I also told them where to run when they hit the ball. While out in the field, I told them that whoever got the ball just needed to throw it to me at the shortstop position, and I would take care of the rest. If this were a team of good baseball players, that strategy would have failed because they would have played the game the way they thought it should be played. The kids on my team didn't know any better, so they did exactly what I asked them to do.

Although we lost one game that week, the team that beat us lost two games, so this group of kids won what might have been the only athletic award they would win in their entire lives. They and their parents were extremely proud as they walked past the best players at camp to receive their ribbons on that Friday night. As I walked by the coach, he just shook his head and asked how I did it. I told him that they did what I asked. Our Coach is the same way; He is glorified when we do what He asks.

This is the same lesson the Israelites had to learn as they crossed over into the Promised Land. When you are in over your head and don't know what to do, just follow the directions. That was God's instructions to the Israelites. The military drills it into its soldiers and coaches of young kids for every sport do the same. For any discipline and for any age, until its participants understand why they need to do something, then they just need to follow instructions.

As knowledge for a particular discipline grows, more complex instructions can be given. Because Moses was trying to wean theological novices from their Egyptian indoctrination, he was limited in what he was able to teach as well as the method by which it was taught. Jesus had a similar problem with trying to educate fishermen about the nature of God. The best illustration pertains to the way the apostle Paul wrote to various churches in different continents. While he could only paint muted word pictures for his once-pagan audience in Corinth, he was able to construct a deep theological message for the church at Rome by using big words like sanctification, justification, and redemption. Certainly God inspired the writing of the Bible, but any words chosen by the authors would have to be at the level of their audiences.

Stretching the Truth

There is no way to count the number of times my parents stretched the truth when I was very young. When I was two years old and curiosity about the kitchen stove would get the best of me, my mom would swat my leg and make me get down as I was about to get up on a chair to investigate. She told me to never touch the stove because it would burn me. However, this was not always true since the stove was rarely on. The same thing happened with water coming out of the faucet and pulling the cords on electrical appliances. I guess I would also have to include the stories they told me about that man in the red suit. They lied about Santa Claus, they lied about the Easter Bunny, and they lied about the tooth fairy. It seems that parents spend a lot of time lying to kids who are very young.

THEY LIED?

I now realize that they really weren't telling lies but rather were just using a little license to get their points across. The use of literary license is a way of stretching the truth by using word pictures and teaching devices to enhance the lessons being explained. These were concepts young minds could not possibly understand without using their five senses to process. When we had children of our own, we decided to stretch the truth as well to teach the same concepts.

Today's teachers have a plethora of instructional tools, such as pictures, videos, chalkboards, textbooks, and computers to get their points across to their students, yet they still struggle to effectively communicate with these young minds. Why would we expect teachers like Moses thousands of years ago to be able to get their points across without also using license? Because Moses was trained in Egypt, he would have learned about hieroglyphics, which is primarily communication through word pictures. Therefore, the stories he shared with the children of Israel were notably vivid word pictures.

Little did he know it, but when Moses struck the rock at Meribah to provide water for the Israelites in the desert instead of speaking to it as God had instructed, it had a profound effect on human history. Worn down by the constant whining of the children of Israel, Moses struck the rock as he had done before at the rock of Horeb to bring forth water and even told us he did it a second time to show it was no accident. By disobeying God, Moses' punishment was that he would not lead the Israelites into the Promised Land but would only get to see it from the top of a nearby mountain. As sad as that would have been for Moses, the reality of him not accompanying them in this military engagement was that all of his knowledge would die with him. Until now, everything had been handed down to each subsequent generation by word of mouth from Adam to the present.

As the Israelites left Egypt and headed for the Promised Land, God gave Moses the Law and instructed him to write it down, as well as the covenant between God and Israel. Interestingly, God never instructed Moses to write down the history of the world as was handed down from Adam, Methuselah, and the rest of the patriarchs. Had he been going into the new land with them, he would have taught them along the way about their history, even during the 38 years of additional wandering. By instructing Moses to write down the Law and the covenant, God was telling Moses to commit to permanent record Israel's story beginning at Abraham and moving forward. Israel would have been familiar with the other patriarchal stories in that there would have been substantial overlap of those Bible characters who lived hundreds of years. For example, Adam would have been alive for about one-fourth of the entire 4,000 years of Bible history, including even being alive during the time of Noah. So how did Moses striking the rock affect so much of human history?

When Moses struck the rock, he was sentenced to die because he disobeyed God. Had he not done this, there would have been no need to write anything else down since he could verbally share everything with them once they crossed over into their new homeland. Because the parents of the children of Israel would not be going into the New Land either, there was nothing to gain by starting a verbal accounting for people not crossing over. Hence, the need for a written record prior to their children's assault on the land they were promised.

While visiting Israel and Egypt a few years ago, we stopped at a store in Cairo where they demonstrated to the visitors how papyrus is made. It was fascinating to watch. By splitting the papyrus plant into thin sheets, overlapping them and letting them dry under pressure, a sheet of papyrus could then be used to write on. It was surprising how long it took to make just one sheet. Consider how many pages there are in the books of Genesis, Exodus, Leviticus, Numbers and Deuteronomy and how few papyrus plants there likely would have been in the desert. It was one thing for Moses to write down the Law and the covenant as he was instructed. It was another thing for Moses to take the time to make enough papyrus to write down the other things that weren't instructed. To do this, he had to be on a mission once informed of his upcoming death. If we knew the date of our death, how urgent and how different would our mission be?

Moses' primary purpose for his writings was to prepare and

inspire the children of Israel for their assault on their new land and to bond them together as teammates. The existing inhabitants of the New Land already had their own gods, just as the Egyptians they left had their own gods. Reinforcing the power of God to these spiritual infants so they could defeat their adversaries would take incredible inspiration from Moses. Ultimately, Moses was trying to teach the children of the children of Israel about the God who had been driven from their collective memory banks through four hundred years of bondage in Egypt. In essence, Moses was that kid pulled from the class.

Moses used a talking serpent to help those novice minds understand the concepts he was presenting to them which is probably where Saturday morning cartoons got the idea to also give animals human characteristics. Throw in a couple of trees with strange names and consequences for Adam and Eve and you have a great instructional word picture from the real garden of Eden, which was bordered by four known rivers. Moses did an exceptional job of teaching those lessons to the children of Israel although, like all word pictures, there were holes in the stories that those novice minds would have never realized. For example, not having to explain how dinosaurs fit into his teachings provided a wider angle from which to teach. In the same way, young children cannot connect the dots on our illustrations either.

Imagine that the events Moses wrote about happened today and instead of the children of Israel coming out of Egypt being theological infants, they all had their Doctorate in Theology degrees from a major university. Would Moses use the same instruction methods for a group so educated as he did for the children of Israel over three thousand years ago? Probably not.

Moses penned the emotional story of God requiring

? WAS THE SERPENT STORY MADE UP,
JUST FOR THE ISREALITES compare?

Abraham to sacrifice his son Isaac on Mount Moriah, which was a three-day journey away. That meant that for three days, Abraham would have to dwell on the death of his son. When Abraham was about to kill Isaac, God stopped him. Moses stated that now God knew Abraham trusted God. It is an incredible story dripping with powerful emotions because it was between a father and his son. Here is another fork in the road to sit and chat about with your young traveling companion. As we read this story about Abraham and Isaac, either God is not omniscient and Moses recorded this story accurately or God is omniscient and Moses used license to construct a great lesson to get his point across to the children of Israel about devotion to God. My vote goes with allowing Moses sufficient latitude to get his points across. How do you see it?

Although it is certainly an infallible book, the Bible is not infallible in the way the religion of Christianity currently teaches it. The Bible is the greatest and most ingenious and inspirational book ever written as its writers drew their inspiration from the Creator of the universe to share stories that would inspire an emotional reaction toward faith in God. However, the license used by these inspired writers allowed them the leeway to make their points at the level of understanding of their intended audience. The sole intent and mission of the book is to teach; that is why we study it. The Bible didn't just fall out of the sky as if God wrote it. God inspired these men to write things that would teach pertinent lessons to their intended audience. Their listeners were typically illiterate, and there were no pictures or chalkboards during the time it was written. The only teaching tool available was word pictures and the miracles to confirm them, as well as the examples of those who came before them.

The whole of Christianity is about managing emotions since emotions unleash God. Christianity was intended to showcase the emotional rollercoaster of believers in an unseen Creator, His Son, and the unbridled power of the human spirit hitched to that wagon. The authors involved in this rollercoaster ride used word pictures to paint as vivid a picture as possible to entice investigation and facilitate learning. After all, wasn't that the purpose in the first place?

Every writer of Scripture used whatever teaching tools were available to make a lasting impression on the minds of his audience by helping them visualize the intended concepts. If there were such a thing as an infallible parent (which there isn't), would that parent still tell his or her young child about Santa Claus? Absolutely.

Master's Degree

Jesus used this same teaching device in His lessons. By utilizing parables, Jesus was able to incorporate stories that may or may not have been true to make the point of the lesson He was teaching to His followers and students. These followers were, by definition of their background, theologically ignorant and illiterate to the point that they actually had to ask Jesus to teach them how to pray (Luke 11:1). They could have never grasped the difficult concepts without using word pictures, metaphors, and parables. License manifests itself through these teaching tools. It is not necessary for these items to be true, but it is important for the teaching device to be believable to be effective.

In the Revelation letter, the apostle John painted a picture at the end of the story of a city with streets paved with gold and all kinds of other precious gems. That certainly would be a metaphoric description of a beautiful city to be longed for, as few people would consider that imagery to represent a factual description of the New Jerusalem. After all, why would the New Jerusalem need walls or a gate? Considering all of the imagery John used in his vision, what actually represented reality and what represented a metaphoric description? How would you explain it?

To us, Jesus was the greatest teacher who ever lived. In saying that, by definition, we have to allow Jesus to use every available teaching aid and device for His message to connect with His audience. We lose the kids of this generation when we put Jesus in a box and do not allow Him full access to novice minds through some of the same teaching methods we use today. When Jesus went into the desert after being baptized, He later taught His followers that Satan tempted Him for forty days while He was in the desert. At this time Jesus had not selected his twelve apostles, so there were no witnesses in the desert.

Here are some other things to consider while walking through the jungle: Were the things written about an evil being tempting Jesus in the desert a metaphoric story or literal details? And does the Bible reveal 100 percent of God's nature, or considering the things we have learned since then, did the Bible's writers only reveal 0.1 percent of God's nature? Or is it somewhere in between? What will be learned about God in the millennia to come?

In His ministry, Jesus used parables numerous times by describing stories that weren't true or accurate to get a specific point across. When Jesus related the parable of the Good Samaritan, it is not important whether those actual events ever took place. Jesus got His message across by painting a word

picture that would have certainly been possible and belie
and would have applied to every member of the audience. Th
is what defines a great teacher.

Moses was the first writer of Scripture, so his students could
only grasp so much information. However, for each subsequent
generation, their teacher would have used an increasing amount
of understanding of God. That is, as people grow in the
knowledge of God, it becomes possible to understand the full
power of His nature. If we were going to gauge how accurately
Moses' writings captured God, on a scale of one to one hundred,
it might only be a five or a seven. That is not to say Moses didn't
completely understand God; it is to say that Moses' audience's
capability of understanding was about that low because of their
Egyptian brainwashing.

If we were going to gauge the accuracy of Jesus' teaching
about God using the same scale, it might be somewhere around
twenty or so. Since Jesus would have known God intimately, we
could say that He had perfect knowledge but could only share
it at the level of His disciples, who were fishermen and a tax
collector. Therefore, their level of understanding dictated Jesus'
methods of instruction.

This brings us back to the previous story about a stove
and a two-year-old. Imagine that a group of thirty-year-olds
are standing around a stove when somebody walks up to the
group and suggests they whip up some eggs for breakfast. One
member of the group tells the visitor they can't cook anything
on the stove because his mother told him not to touch the stove.
The visitor asks when that took place, and the guy responds that
it was when he was two years old. It resembles what is currently
taking place in the church. It is as if we recorded everything our

s as two-year-olds, wrote them in a book, and
 live by them.

f every author of Scripture were written to a
 for a specific place at a specific time. Let's
 these teachers be the great teachers they were by letting
them transmit their message to their own audience first before
considering what their words might mean to us. The clues for
unlocking the treasure are found in the words of these incredible
writers. Interpreting their words in the way they were intended
will light the way for every generation that follows.

CHAPTER 6

Education Overhaul

Long before a child is born, there are certain things that child is destined to do based on the parents' set of values or priorities. These mandates will likely include things like eating their vegetables, doing their homework, taking piano lessons, going to church, etc. A child's obligation to replicate his or her parents' values will eventually end either through self-sufficiency or at their college dorm room, whichever comes first. While our children are growing up under our roofs, we diligently try to instill our values in them so that once they are on their own they will have a foundation for the life they might choose. If we have gone to church every time the doors were open, then we expect them to do the same throughout their lives. It is as if we expect the Pavlovian principles our parents fed us to also work on our kids. But it doesn't, not for this generation. Children born in this Internet age are being fed far more information from numerous contrarian sources that counterbalance their previous beliefs, making conditioned responses nearly impossible.

Each religious group within Christianity is differentiated

m another by their Scriptural interpretation related to what they think is literal and what they think is figurative. That is, each group determines what they believe from the Bible based on what they think is real and what they think is a story. In turn, the doctrinal differences between groups, by definition, affect how the Bible is taught in each group in our religious culture today. Because there are dozens of different denominations (for lack of a better word), it would stand to reason that, statistically speaking, one group might stand head and shoulders above the rest related to the resonance of faith of their young people as they go out into the world. Surely, out of all these different philosophies, theologies, and doctrines, there is one interpretation of Scripture able to galvanize the faith of teenagers. Unfortunately, that is not the case.

From my research, there is not a single group in Christianity that is immune to the disintegration of faith among their young people. Certainly, some groups do a better job entertaining their youth so that they are able to corral them before they go off to engage in spiritual warfare. However, the evaporation rate upon leaving home seems to be approximately the same for just about all religious groups.

Regardless of the group in this day and time, any interpretation of Scripture based solely on heritage will not survive in the minds of its youth. The church's teachings of the Bible do not provide sufficient evidence that God exists, much less demonstrate the available horsepower that faith provides. All it will take to set the faith of our teenagers on fire and sustain them is to transform the Bible's teachings into a platform for demonstrating God's available power in their lives. Change is hard but watching our children leave the churc not able to fortify their faith is even harder.

Introduction to God

Of the hundreds of characters described in th one character in particular that we know the least about. This character is listed in every book of the Bible with the exception of *Esther* and is given preferential treatment by all of its writers. He is described with just about every adjective the writers could think of while still never even approaching His nature. He is called by many names and descriptions, and there are no limits to His incredible power. Despite all that, the Bible character that we know the least about is God.

When you think about it, all we have ever heard about God is what He is like rather than what He is. Although we are made in God's invisible spiritual image (Col. 1:15), God has no physical image for us to be like. Think of it this way: if God were lost and you were going to put His picture on a telephone pole or a milk carton, what would that picture look like? If you were going to sit down with a sketch artist to help him draw a picture of God, what characteristics would you use so people would know Him when they found Him?

CHRIST IS THE IMAGE OF THE INVISIBLE GOD.

How would you answer the following questions:

+ How big is God?
+ How tall is God?
+ Does He have arms and legs?
+ What does He sound like? Biologically, how does He make a sound?
+ Where is He? What are His coordinates?

Does His hair have to be cut? What color is it?

- ✦ What does it mean to be made in His image?
- ✦ Does He have ears? Why would an omniscient God need to hear anything?

In order to unleash His power, the first thing we have to understand is that God is not a person. Teaching that God is a person is one of the fatal flaws in the church's teachings because it limits His power while people who believe such a thing cannot explain the details of their thought process. There is not a square inch for trillions of light years in all directions that God does not inhabit. He does not have any human attributes, no matter how many the inspired writers of scripture gave Him to illustrate their points. It is we, as humans, who should emulate God's attributes and not the other way around.

The teaching device people use to help them understand God is called *personification*. Assigning human characteristics to non-human things makes it easier for people to grasp things that would have been difficult to understand otherwise. This same training method is used in every children's worship training session for young children through puppetry to help them understand the lessons being taught. Actually, it works so well that companies doing Saturday-morning cartoons have made a mint utilizing personification. By watching coyotes go off to work or dogs drive cars or bears read books to their children and cook a meal, it is easier for children to understand the concepts being presented. When you think about it, Jesus came to personify God for people of faith so they could put a face with a name.

Moses understood God one way based on his life experiences,

and Job understood Him another way based on hi

So did Isaiah, Jeremiah, Elijah, Paul, Barnabas an

God is the same yesterday, today and forever

He doesn't change, our understanding of God shou...

each time we encounter Him as our knowledge changes and

increases. ___

About thirteen hundred years elapsed from the time Moses descended Mt. Sinai with the Ten Commandments to the time Jesus ascended a similar mountain to begin his teaching ministry. Although some people might say that Jesus changed many of the things Moses taught related to rituals and service to God in His teachings, Jesus did not actually change a single thing taught by Moses during his entire three year ministry. As He said in Matt 5:17, He did not come to abolish the Law, He came to fulfill it. That is, He came to reset the trajectory of faith and understanding of God to where thirteen hundred years of experiencing God should have taken it. ___

In the same way that Algebra and Calculus do not contradict arithmetic but rather are progressions from it, Jesus' teachings were simply the natural progression of the things Moses taught the children of Israel in the desert. Moses' teachings laid the foundation of faith and devotion to God; Jesus built upon them by highlighting the things they should have already extrapolated from thirteen hundred years of experiencing God. For example, Moses taught the children of Israel that they were not to commit adultery; Jesus went a step farther and taught them not to lust. At some point in time between Moses and Jesus, their understanding of God should have evolved from the disciplinarian God necessary for the children of Israel to reclaim their land to the God of Love. Because that transition was slow

. coming, it made Jesus' teachings more controversial than they should have been.

Are we perhaps guilty of the same thing today? Has our understanding of God been just as slow to evolve? Our teachings today continue to personify God the same way Moses did 3,300 years ago instead of growing in the knowledge of God as Peter and Paul instructed. That has created a dichotomy where doctrine has been incapable of keeping pace with the world's discoveries. When dinosaurs were unearthed and Homo sapiens fossils discovered that were carbon dated to be tens of thousands of years old, some people thought that contradicted Scripture. To the contrary, these discoveries actually reveal God's enormous power at creation. Reconciling science books with God's Word by using one to explain the other makes it a lot easier for teenagers to believe. On the other hand, when people of faith do misguided things like sell all their possessions awaiting Jesus' return on specific calendar dates, it undermines young people's faith instead of strengthening it. After all, who wants to be part of a group of people noted for having their heads in the sand?

The sole purpose for presenting a Bible class is to equip the audience with tools they did not have before the class started. If the goal is to find hidden spiritual treasures, then the purpose for having the class in the first place is to hand out spiritual shovels to accomplish that goal. There are four components in the presentation of a Bible lesson that should be present during every sermon or lesson to help the audience grow:

+ It must be interesting
+ It must be relevant

+ It must be memorable
+ It must emotionally connect with everyone in the audience.

All of Jesus' teachings had these ingredients in His lessons, but His parables notably highlighted these attributes in more focus and detail. Every single lesson Jesus ever taught was enveloped with emotions so strong that He could effect change in a person's life with His first encounter. When He taught about a man who was robbed and beaten on the road to Jericho while noting that a priest and Levite passed him by and a Samaritan chose to help him, Jesus was invoking any number of emotions from His audience. Utilizing contemporary details in His stories made them interesting to His audience while making His points so they would not be soon forgotten. It is impossible for people today, especially young people, to comprehend the magnitude of the images Jesus created in His parables. Anyone who has lived in a city their entire life will have a hard time extracting life lessons from biblical word pictures related to farming and tending sheep. Every lesson from scripture must be carefully weighed for its emotional quotient and then transformed into relevant modern word pictures to carry the intended spiritual weight.

The most effective way to teach the Bible is to present its lessons and parables as they are written as well as presenting a parallel story that replicates the emotions of those lessons seen through the prism of life today. Telling stories to a class of young people about swords, kings and cultures they are not emotionally connected with will make them associate Bible study with irrelevance or boredom. These stories should always be told with a modern twist to keep people emotionally engaged. That

WHERE THEY NOT WRITING THE THINGS THAT GOD PUT ON THEIR HEARTS TO WRITE.

WHAT ABOUT OUR FAITH IN THE INSPIRATION OF THE AUTHORS?

puts the responsibility squarely on the shoulders of Bible teachers of mining for every emotion intended for the original audience.

I'm sure you have heard of the story of the six blind men and the elephant where the six blind men feel different parts of the elephant. They then each give a completely different account of the same elephant because their perspective is different than the rest. In the Bible, the writers of Scripture gave us their own perspective of God from their vantage point, and just like the blind men, they gave completely different descriptions of God. Anyone who has ever tried to work a jigsaw puzzle without a picture to go by can understand the limitations of these writers. That is why the only way to see God's picture is to put the entire puzzle together from each of their individual perspectives and to view it from the distance that time creates.

As we see things from their vantage point, imagine how much less the Bible authors would have known about God in their limited worldview. While they would have looked at the moon with awe, we have actually visited it and seen more distant stars, planets, and galaxies than they could have imagined. That is how we are able to fill in some of the missing information about God. Because our faith is the limiting factor for accessing God's power, the authors of the Bible shrank God for their audience so they could get their arms around Him.

Love Is God

"For God so loved the world that He gave His only begotten Son" (John 3:16 NIV). In the third and fourth chapters of John's gospel, as well as his other letters, John seems to be focusing his audience's attention, through the retelling of Jesus' conversation with Nicodemus and the woman at the well, on these thoughts: God is Spirit, God is love, and spiritual love knows no boundaries. It had likely been about fifty years since Jesus' death and resurrection when John recounted these and other stories that the other gospel writers omitted. None of the other writers mentioned Nicodemus by name and certainly not the details of this story as Jesus talked about God's love with Nicodemus. Nor did these other writers acknowledge Jesus and the disciples' pit stop in Samaria when Jesus asked a Samaritan woman for a drink of water.

This is the first time Jesus taught that God is Spirit, or at least the first time someone thought it important enough to be written down. A lot of things changed when the Roman Empire destroyed Jerusalem. This might have driven John into the same Gentile cities where Paul had been, giving him a different perspective, which is noted in the stories he included. Although Mark only mentioned the word *love* in a couple of incidents in his gospel, John laced love in most stories he told, from Jesus' love for Lazarus causing tears to flow to showing them "the full extent of His love" (John 13:1 NIV) by washing the apostles' feet. As John recounted those special days, he remembered how much Jesus loved him by His words and His actions. That is how others know of our love as well.

In today's world, the word *love* barely resembles its original intent. In this culture, as we try to teach our kids about the love of God, love has become more of a slogan or an off-handed remark than a commitment of spirit. This makes it harder to equate God with love, as John did. We have all heard some of these phrases or comments: I love ice cream; I love pizza; I love hamburgers; I love your hair; I love your dress; I love New York; I love a good steak; and of course: I love you, whatever our culture now deems that to mean. In the past few years, someone came up with the phrase *unconditional love* to try and differentiate one love from another, as if there is such a thing as conditional love. But I guess it is conditional if while the TV is working it is loved but when it is broken it is not. It's a good thing that being broken and being loved are not mutually exclusive related to people.

So what is the definition of love? From cover to cover, the Bible takes great care in defining love as it describes God and His infinite love, but somewhere in time, Paul's description in 1 Corinthians 13 of how the Corinthians should try to get along in their dysfunctional congregation became the marquee definition of love. Although it is not a comprehensive list, it describes the similarities between love and God. This passage may not define the complexities of God or love but it does provide a glimpse into both since they are one and the same. When you have defined God, you have defined love.

Although each author painted a different picture of God from their own perspective, they all basically used the same language in their descriptions of the Creator of the Universe and the source of His power: Love. Moses told the children of Israel to love the Lord their God with all their heart, soul, strength, and mind. David tried to quantify the love of God in his psalms but his frustration bled through his writings regarding a lack of adjectives descriptive enough to capture the essence of God. And at the end of the first century, John encapsulated what each of them had been trying to express so inadequately by equating God with Love itself.

Therefore, the love of God is an ocean in which we are trying to immerse ourselves. The words of inspired authors instruct

us to love our neighbors, our enemies, each other, our fam
and ourselves so there is no misunderstanding about how dee
and penetrating this ocean is to be in our lives. As love grows, it
soaks everything indiscriminately just as a rising ocean tide will
bury everything in its wake. That is, if we love our families, we
will also love our co-workers and our bosses, as well as the guy
who cut us off at the traffic light, the same. Love is not capable
of picking and choosing where it breaks out. If we would go into
a burning building to save our children one day, we would go
into a burning building the next day to save someone we don't
even know. Love stains without prejudice; we just have to keep
growing in God and in Love to one day get there.

Wherever God is, there is love and vice versa. Just as God
has no boundaries, neither does love, nor hope, nor joy, etc.
They are all spiritual entities, so they have no boundaries, which
sometimes can be difficult to understand. Someone who lives
beside a power plant has plenty of available power to draw from;
he only has to believe it is available and plug into that power.

The God of Creation

We actually owe much of what we know about God to the arena
of science. It is important to remember that nothing that has
ever been discovered or uncovered contradicts a single word of
Scripture. In fact, every new piece of information reveals another
pixel in the portrait of God that wasn't available thousands of
years ago. Although many scientists may in fact be atheists,
they unknowingly have provided Christians with a better view
of God than we could have ever seen on our own. For example,
astronomy has provided us with some incredible pictures and
dimensions of God's power at creation that we could have never

t these images. In addition, archeologists have
s of ancient civilizations while paleontologists
the fossils of prehistoric animals that fill in
zzle pieces for interpreting Scripture. For me,
when scientists unraveled clues to the human genome, it was
like watching a video of God at work at creation.

The most important scientific discoveries that have
illuminated the awesomeness of God come in the fields of biology
and neuroscience. The authors who penned the Bible had no
clue about the intricate design of the brain and its functions
relating to God's interaction with mankind. As we will see,
when Moses instructed the Israelites to love the Lord their God
with all their heart, soul, strength, and mind, unknown to him,
he was instructing them to use the full measure of their minds to
try to encounter God. Much of the Law was based on following
God's nature from a biological point of view.

Some people might have trouble understanding how an
omniscient spiritual being could throw a bunch of rocks in all
directions so they all spin in some designed orchestration. I
get that. However, there is no way any intelligent person could
believe the human body was just made from scratch and come
up with any other conclusion than that this did not just happen.
Another thing that would tend to blow apart the big bang
theory is that heavenly bodies are typically round or spherical
in composition. Things that break apart from something else do
not tend to become round.

To think that the human male body, with its brain's tens
of millions of interrelated cells and numerous body functions,
happened to evolve at the same time and cadence and exactly
opposite the human female body's time and cadence is statistically

impossible in any game of chance. The odds for some[...] like that happening on its own would be like shooting a gu[...] in one direction and hoping it hits a target across the ocean in the other direction. Some people may say it was intelligent design that created the heavens and the earth and all that is in it; people of faith just call this life-creating force God. We may not understand God as we should, but believing otherwise is a far greater leap of faith. Once a person believes that the human body is an incredibly designed piece of equipment that could have originated from nothing other than God, then believing the rest of the story about rotating rocks becomes a whole lot easier.

To the degree that science has done most of the heavy lifting regarding our ability to understand God in His proper context, they deserve our appreciation and anticipation of discoveries to come. While many scientists believe their work may dissolve faith in God, the discoveries to be made over the millions of years to come will only bring God's power into clearer focus. It is mind numbing to consider what we have learned about God just in our lifetime. Imagine what will be learned about God through the eyes of space and science in the years to come. God inspired these writers to write things to their audience for whatever specific reasons prompted them to write in the first place. Trying to frame relevance out of those words thousands of years later with all that has changed about the world without placing the letter back in its original mailbox defies logic.

Letters from Home

Imagine that a letter you wrote to someone was found two thousand years from now. There would certainly be aspects of that correspondence that would be misunderstood by the

First of all, they probably wouldn't know what ⌐ if you mentioned in the letter that you had ⌐ all to find something, they probably wouldn't ⌐ all was or why someone would need to drive to get an⌐ ⌐o learn what your letter was about, they would have to dig through ancient archives to learn about letters, malls, and perhaps even about driving to make any sense of what you were relating in your correspondence. Unfortunately, there is little archived information from two thousand years ago, but that does not diminish the requirement to get inside the minds of those who wrote the letters to uncover the true intent of their words.

God's power is unlimited. If we want to try to get our arms around what the boundaries of *unlimited* are, we should start by considering things that telescopes millions of years from now will discover that will prove what God made in the beginning. Once we allow that information to wash over our minds and souls, we can begin to understand that the boundaries of the possibilities for our lives and the lives of everyone we come in contact with are the same boundaries of the nature of God. All it takes to tap into that power is to simply believe it is there, like plugging into an electrical socket. It only takes a sold-out faith in God to access all of the benefits that being like Him creates.

CHAPTER 7

The Purpose of the Church

Christianity is a team sport.

The word *church* has different meanings depending on the perspective being considered, which adds another layer of confusion for young people to sort through. Sometimes it refers to a building while other times it pertains to a group of people. In either case, the word has negative connotations among young people because it is associated with things you have to do instead of things you get to do. Few people actually know what the purpose of the church is.

Let's identify the purpose of the church by first identifying what it is not. When the "roll is called up yonder," there won't be any churches called, just individuals. Now stop and mull that over for a moment. Everything we do in the church as a group of believers is supposed to propel us toward standing on our own. Therefore, before getting caught up in all of the things congregations typically fuss about, the first order of business for the church should be to figure out its purpose. Why did Jesus "build" His church in the first place? The fact that many of us drive by several other churches on the way to our own, or that billions of dollars may have been spent on land and buildings to accomplish the same thing screams that we may not understand why Jesus built the church.

First of all, nowhere in the New Testament does it even say that we are to gather to "worship" God other than the vague reference in Hebrews reminding the audience of their former discipline. That doesn't mean that we aren't supposed to do it; in fact, it would be foolish to do otherwise. It just means that it was never intended to be part of a religious exercise. There is inordinate value for a group of people who believe unbelievable things to come together as a family to share how that faith has impacted their lives. However, executing a series of rituals as part of a worship service will not help us communicate with God or in any way augment our preparation for spiritual warfare.

Any company or organization worth its salt will likely have some type of mission statement to guide its activities. Its inception would have certainly been based on somebody's vision or mission to accomplish something so committing that mission to words would be a way to focus attention on the core beliefs or values of that particular group. As an example, a company that makes widgets might have a mission statement that includes wording about the intended quality of the widget being made as well as the working conditions and welfare of its employees. It might also include its intent on taking care of the environment in the manufacturing process. Of course, unless the widget can be sold at a profit all of this would be a moot point. Determining what a group's mission really should be can get lost in the process of trying to define it. Jesus was a man on a mission. Once His ministry began, each of the gospel writers noted how focused He was toward accomplishing that mission. Even His closest followers didn't actually understand His mission even though He clearly defined it at every point along the way. Had His followers been asked to write a mission statement of what they thought they were trying to accomplish, they would have likely included things like wresting control of Israel from the Romans and returning Israel to its glory. Even after Jesus' death and resurrection and as Jesus was about to ascend into heaven, the apostles still asked about their mission.

Understanding the purpose of the church is not hard, but it may require that we unlearn almost everything we thought we knew about the religion of Christianity in order to decipher the treasure's clues. The sole purpose of the church is SYNERGY; that is, whatever faith might be generated on our own would be far less than when supported by each other. After all, it is impossible to circle the wagons with only one wagon. There is strength in numbers in numerous activities and reinforcing faith in an unseen God would be at the top of that list. When Peter was in the midst of Jesus and the other apostles before Jesus' arrest, he was wielding his sword against a large group of seasoned soldiers but once he was without his wingmen, it only took a servant girl to puncture his faith. The church was established simply to be a conduit for synergy by establishing a direct connection between believers, accentuating the flow of spiritual fuel that can set faith on fire. When Solomon noted that "a cord of three strands is not easily broken (Ecclesiastes 4:12 NIV), he unknowingly described the purpose of the church.

Running on Empty
Do you ever feel like you are running on empty? Do you ever feel that you are just going through the motions at church while your faith gauge shows there is nothing left in the tank? The interesting thing is that when a car runs out of gas, it stops

dead in its tracks. However, people who run out of gas can still live their lives as if nothing is wrong. After all, faith is not required for hearts to beat and brains to function. You can go to school and still try to be popular without having faith, just like many adults can raise their children while pretending to have good relationships with their friends and family even though their patience and self-control may have run out. One of the most important things to understand about faith is that it is impossible to live by faith while running on fumes.

When you think about it, people can go to church every time the doors are open and even sing the songs and pray the prayers without anyone ever knowing that their faith has left the building. After all, faith is not a requirement for attending church. In fact, there is not a single action or activity in the church that requires it. Let me say that again: there is not a single action or activity in the church that requires faith. Although the sole foundation upon which the power of God is launched and shared is faith, it is not a required component of participating in things that define the church.

For example, a person can preach or teach while having an affair or an addiction. A person can lead the most elegant prayer or perfectly sing the most spiritual song or even take communion without having to expose their disbelief or doubt. In Christianity, many times we talk about the importance of faith with our children but then never go through the biology of how it is attained or generated. That is like a football coach trying to get his team ready for a game without having a football.

At its inception, the church was constructed to be a filling station of faith for all who attend. Somewhere in time it became a religion that essentially shut down its pumps. When the church

isn't able to fill all of its members every time they
the church, by definition, hasn't fulfilled its so'
existence. The only way for our faith to grow and our ᵕ
to get recharged is by tapping into God's Spirit, and for that to
happen, someone has to care enough to read faces and emotions
and then share God accordingly. After all, that is where the fuel
is stored and the treasure is buried.

We have all had times when we pull into the church parking
lot looking to be filled with God's grace and power but leave just as
empty as we arrived. That really should never happen since Jesus'
teachings are intended to be a source of renewable and perpetual
energy. That is supposed to make us different, but unfortunately,
statistics show that not to be the case. Christians probably take up
as much couch time in the counselor's or psychiatrist's office as the
rest of the world, and even though we give lip service to treating our
bodies as the temple of God, we have many of the same addictions
as everyone else. We live like the world, we dress like the world,
we drink like the world, we eat like the world, and we watch what
the world watches. That is why we have the same problems as the
rest of the world. People who continually come to church but leave
just as empty as when they came will eventually leave to find some
other source of fuel, no matter how contaminated it might be.

Follow the Leader

There are two things that come to mind to illustrate how the
church should function. The first way is by equating the church
with an athletic team's training because training routines and
methods are nearly the same for all sports. Young athletes train
one way while older athletes train another, which is also true
in the church. The essential element for each group is that by

raining together, they will push each other to become stronger than they would have by themselves.

The second way is called *drafting* in auto racing, when one car runs directly behind another car so it rides in the slipstream of the car in front of it. In this configuration, the car in back doesn't have to penetrate the air and other dynamics of physics like the front car does. Although the church is certainly not a competition, it is about spiritually strong people leading the pack so others can draft off of their strengths during their training. Combining teamwork and drafting creates a special combination for use by followers of God. Teamwork on the ball field, drafting on a race track, and other synergistic activities like creating wind under a person's sails all illustrate the available power of the church.

We don't come together to please God; just saying that undermines His power. We come together to draw strength from each other and do whatever it takes to grow in God's likeness and then utilize those talents to alter the lives of as many people as possible. Because imitation is the sincerest form of flattery, God is glorified when we do everything possible to resemble His nature. People who show others where the land mines are buried are leaders in the church simply because that encourages other people to follow, whether men or women. That enables them to run the race of life with more speed and confidence.

Caesarea Philippi

A tour of the Holy Land **is** an incredible asset for growing faith. No matter how many times a person has read through the Bible, seeing the actual places where Jesus walked and lived certainly provides a different perspective than just reading about them in a book. The best way I can relate what it was like to experience the places where many of the events in the Bible took place as opposed to just reading about them is like watching a high definition digital movie versus black and white photos. Whether walking the streets of Jerusalem, riding in a boat across the Sea of Galilee, or standing in the ruins of the very synagogue in Capernaum where Jesus taught, correlating the things that are seen with the stories that were told certainly leaves an indelible mark on believers. Obviously, there were no videos of the events that occurred at those locations nearly two thousand years ago, so some of the emotional effect was lost as time changed the backdrop. Even so, the story of Jesus and His disciples passing through the region of Caesarea Philippi jumps off the page as you see for yourself what prompted Jesus' discussion about the church with His disciples in the first place.

Caesarea Philippi
(Photograph by Jennifer McMurtry)

Caesarea Philippi was a pagan town, with its backdrop being a small mountain of stone with caves cut out of the rock at its base to honor the Greek god of nature, Pan. It is not hard to picture the wild parties held to honor Pan at the base of this mountain with its noise reverberating off the stone. Peter's name up to now was Simon, son of Jonah. With that word picture in mind as the setting for an important discussion between Jesus and His disciples, consider the conversation.

Jesus first asked His disciples who others thought He was. He then asked who they thought He was. Simon acknowledged his belief that Jesus was the Christ, the Son of God, which is exactly what we acknowledge to each other as believers of the same thing. It is Jesus' response to that, absent an understanding of the backstory, that has been totally misconstrued. Jesus used their knowledge about Caesarea Philippi to create a mental photograph that would be burned into their memory banks for the rest of their lives.

Jesus created a word play about Caesarea Philippi's main attraction: the rock of Pan. Jesus told Simon that because of his acknowledgment of Jesus' power, Simon's name became Cephas or Peter, meaning "rock," and that He would build a team based on that power as the Son of God. That's starting a team with a pretty good pitcher and clean-up hitter. While standing on the opponents' home field, He threw down the gauntlet to inspire His teammates: you will become so strong that you will be able to defeat even these guys devoted to their pagan god, Pan. "And the gates of hell shall not prevail" (Matt. 16:18 ESV). It is as if Jesus was giving his team a pregame pep talk. That had to be an incredibly emotional moment for His troops.

To me the greatest basketball player who ever lived is

Michael Jordan. From my point of view, it was not vertical leap, shooting ability, or defensive skills that v greatest attribute. These were great, but a lot of peopl had those individual talents as well. Jordan's greatest attribute was his ability to push his fellow players to find other gears they didn't think they had. He won six NBA championships, and who knows how many more he would have won had he not retired.

Different players were involved in each of those championships. Some left or retired while new players came on board. Imagine that Michael Jordan found the fountain of youth and perpetually played basketball for hundreds of years at his peak performance level. Each year two new players would join the team while two others retired and so on for centuries as they continued to win championships. This is exactly the scenario Jesus was describing to His disciples at Caesarea Philippi. Jesus would perpetually captain His team until the end of time as new people would join the team while others would pass on. Whatever thought or perception you have about the church and all of its rituals and baggage, this is the imagery Jesus seems to have created for His followers, His team. It is important to remember that the purpose of Christianity is that for every choice we have to make, we will be assisted in making the one that most resembles God through the strength our teammates provide. It is intended to be a means to an end rather than just being an end itself.

What Jesus started was His *ekklesia*. I'm not sure how *church* was translated from *ekklesia*, but *team* seems to be the mental picture He was painting, or at least that is the word picture that seems best suited to our culture. These are some of the attributes of teammates: they lift each other up to be and do more than they can do by themselves, they push each other, they console each other, they bear with each other, they teach each other, they train each other, they praise each other, and they correct each other. Each of these attributes and dozens more define the concept of the team as well as the church.

The church is a lot like any team. Although we are all individuals with our own strengths and weaknesses, and although we are all dealing with our own struggles out in the world, we all share a common goal, a common adversary, a common hope, a common love. And yes, we are to work hard when we are not together as a team, trying to do the right things and strive to live godly lives by doing things that help us grow even while we are on our own. The purpose of the church is to create synergy among its members while encouraging the members to be more than they would be by themselves. We may all be called upon to account for our own lives, but since there is strength in numbers, it is a lot easier to make the right choice in the presence of accountability.

Several years ago, my neighbor and I were regularly playing basketball together in pickup games, but we knew that we really needed to get in better shape or we would regret it. We agreed to meet in his garage at 6:00 a.m. on Mondays, Wednesdays, and Fridays to work out for forty-five minutes before going to work. Of course, we were excited to get started. The first day went by smoothly, as did the second day. By the third day, when the clock hit 5:45 a.m., I really wanted to go back to bed. However, knowing a buddy would be waiting on me was all it took to roll out of bed and make it in time for the workout. It turns out he had the same thoughts, but by pushing each other, we continued the workouts that would have never occurred if left to our own volition. That should be how the church works as well.

When everyone is hitting on all cylinders, the rising tide of God's Spirit will lift all boats. The synergy created when hundreds of people are rowing the boat in the same direction will have a ripple effect, prompting more people to get on board.

CHAPTER 8

Mind Management

All people who enjoy watching sports will certainly have seen their share of unbelievable if not miraculous game-ending plays for just about any sport ever played. For football fans, it might be Franco Harris's "immaculate reception" on Christmas Day or the Music City miracle the Tennessee Titans pulled off to defeat the Buffalo Bills. For basketball fans it might be Christian Laettner's basket for Duke to defeat Kentucky in the NCAA tournament. However, the defeat of the Russian hockey team by the United States's hockey team in the 1980 Winter Olympics would have to be at the top of anyone's list of unbelievable victories as Al Michaels's call at the end of that game reminded everyone of its improbability: "Do you believe in miracles?"

Obviously, these plays and games weren't actually miracles. They were certainly incredible plays where preparation and adrenalin met an opportunity, but they probably wouldn't fall into the miracle category, like when a baby is born. The difference between the two is that one is expected and the other isn't. Even though a baby's birth is the most incredible miracle ever performed on earth, because it happens millions of times each year and there are nine months to prepare for its inevitability, nobody lumps it in a group with raising someone from the dead or feeding five thousand people with five loaves and two fish. It is too common for us to be shocked by its occurrence. On the other hand, when a series of events too irrational to believe happens on the gridiron or hard court, the word *miracle* crosses people's lips.

For humans, the things that define miracles are that they have to be unexpected and they have to defy logic. It is pertinent to remember that God doesn't know what a miracle is. That is, God doesn't have a special bag He reaches for whenever something special is needed. Everything that God does is just God being God, with nothing ever done outside the realm of His nature. Whether it involves the events in David's life that prepared him to confront Goliath or an athlete who refuses to accept obvious defeat and then leads his team to victory, they are both born of the same mindset: no boundaries.

In the 2001 US Open, Retief Goosen stood over a two-foot putt to win this prestigious golf tournament. Goosen had played and putted incredibly well the entire tournament, so this putt should have been easy. In fact, on any other day, he probably could have made the putt blindfolded. However, the pressure of the situation seemed to affect his focus and his putting stroke so that he missed this short putt. He had to come back the next day and win the tournament in a playoff while his opponent experienced his own share of pressure. Goosen actually won the same tournament a few years later, absent the pressure of trying to win his first major tournament. In golf history, there have been numerous short putts missed that would have won tournaments by players who had never won before. What makes professional golfers miss these short putts? What gives weekend golfers the yips and shanks while playing a $2 Nassau with their buddies when they don't have those problems when they are playing by themselves? It is from the pressure placed on themselves as their brains try to process numerous thoughts all at the same time.

Whether it involves heaving a ball seventy yards down the field to win a game or missing a two-foot putt or anything in between, there are two main ingredients that are part of that success or failure. Those two ingredients are focus and adrenalin. Focus provides the directional control of any activity while adrenalin provides the velocity. One is the compass while the other is the accelerator pedal. Those two things are part of just about every story in the Bible. That is because focus is an attribute of God while adrenalin is the mind's direct connection with God. The mind has no boundaries and neither does adrenalin. In fact, boundaries and adrenalin are mutually exclusive. Acknowledging boundaries puts the flood back in its bank. The mother who lifts a car off of her child would lose her power if she ever stopped to think whether she could actually do it.

Mental Gymnastics

Neuroscience is the correlation between the mind and body, so Christianity should be at the forefront of understanding this science since that is how God can be unleashed. How we manage focus and adrenalin dictates whether our lives are full of missed putts or touchdown passes and whether the people in our lives can see God in the things we do. Had Peter been able to stay

focused while walking on the water, he wouldn't hav
a lifeline when the distractions came into view. There
no faith where there is no focus. Faith is the ability to tu
distractions by properly assigning value to those distractions.

Moses told the children of Israel what they needed to do to please God. In effect, they were to follow the rules even if they thought about doing something else or thought what they were told to do was wrong. As long as they didn't pick up sticks on the Sabbath and performed the prescribed sacrifices as they were instructed, then they weren't breaking any laws, whether they thought about doing it or not. It is irrelevant whether a small child understands why she shouldn't stick a fork in an electrical outlet; it is only important that she does as she is told to protect her from her own ignorance.

Aviation involves forcing the mind to perform numerous functions at the same time while never letting any of those functions slip through the cracks. A pilot doing ninety-nine percent of the things on his plate perfectly can still end in disaster. One of the first exercises that student pilots undergo involves mind control. At some point in the instruction process, the instructor will take control of the airplane and tell the student pilot to close his or her eyes while the instructor puts the plane into a steep bank. Even with eyes closed, the student's body can feel the pressure created by such a banking action. However, unknown to the student, by remaining in this steep bank a person's body will adjust to this environment and will tell the mind that the plane must have leveled its wings. The instructor will then turn the plane back in a steep bank the other way, bringing the plane back to straight and level. Since the student's body and mind think they were already in level flight, as soon as they feel the airplane banking the other direction, their mind is telling them that they are, again, in a steep bank. As the instructor immediately has the student open their eyes to see that their mind was lying to them, they can see they are in level flight instead of being steeply banked. A pilot learns quickly in his training that the mind can be fooled; the sooner Christians learn that, the less damage to their lives will occur.

Notice how almost all of Jesus' teachings involved the mind while Moses' teachings predominantly involved the body. Jesus took the things that the children of Israel were supposed to do and updated them by highlighting the mind's intended involvement in their execution. In effect, Jesus came to implement a mind management program whereby God's followers would be able to enjoy the benefits of God's power in their lives not limited by rules and regulations. Rules and regulations are necessary components of life and religion in the absence of knowledge and understanding. That is why parents, when asked by their children why they have to do something they don't understand, have patented the phrase "because I said so." In the desert, God did the same.

The children of Israel were instructed to fear God because that would protect them. Since fear is a learned response rather than something loaded into our hard drives at birth, they had to learn what it meant to fear God. Moses was able to foster this protective bubble for them just as parents do today by warning their children what to do and not to do, even absent their understanding of why they were to do it. For example, I am afraid of many things. Snakes, spiders, alligators, etc., are on my list of things to stay away from. When I see people on television handling these creatures without any fear, it blows my mind. These guys don't fear these creatures; however, they do respect the danger associated with handling them, so they use their knowledge of them to access them. Now imagine a life completely absent of fear. Having a healthy respect for the things that can harm us and acting accordingly to avoid them is also something that occurs in the mind in the arena of knowledge. Knowledge destroys fear. Knowledge creates respect.

Mind over Matter

Let me state what should be obvious: God intersects with man solely in the mind. Where else could it be? To make sense of this, just imagine that everything on your body was amputated that could be amputated while you could still live and that every organ was transplanted that could be transplanted. That basically leaves the brain for God and the soul to reside in, even though it is a spiritual occupation rather than anything physical. God is love. Where does love reside? God is spirit. Where does spirit reside? Jesus came to implement this mind management program to provide a more-detailed picture of God. This mental approach can inoculate believers and minimize the bad things that might happen as they discover the full measure of the power of God. It is not intended to end the bad things that might happen but rather to make us a smaller target.

The idea is that since humans typically use only about 10 percent of their brain's firepower, the other 90 percent would make a great home for God to reside. Imagine a life with God biologically in control of the throttle and navigation system after having already knocked down the walls of impossible. I believe that is the idea behind Jesus' teachings. After all, the most unlimited thing on earth is the human mind. At the same time, it is also the most underutilized thing. Since God is unlimited, it is as if He was building a home for Himself when He created us.

Every encounter we have with God on any level begins in our minds. Because God resides in the mind, Christianity is not about what we say or do; it is about what we think that affects what we say or do. The Bible writers had limited biological information to share with their audience. They simply processed existing knowledge in a format that would lead their audience toward a better understanding of God. Even so, if they magically possessed knowledge from millions of years ahead of their time, it would not have changed a single word of their discourse.

Contrary to the things Moses was taught in Egypt about the heart being the seat of the soul, which he passed on through his writings, the mind defines who a person is and not the heart. The heart just pumps blood. In effect, a broken heart is simply an emotional concussion where one side of the brain tries to convince the other side of the brain things that aren't true. Although there wouldn't be anything romantic about giving someone a Valentine's Day card with a picture of a brain on it, that is exactly where every emotion originates. Actually, it is where God, who is love and the source of all emotions, resides. It is also where confidence, panic, despair, joy, love, fear, temptation, self-esteem, and anything else that involves our lives originates.

Learning to Focus
If we were to do a brain scan on David from the time he tended sheep to the time he stood over Goliath in victory, we would be able to see the brain's activity during that time. We could

watch him take target practice and develop into a grea
man while passing the time tending sheep. We could wat
adrenalin saturate his soul as he ran down and killed a lio
a bear to save his sheep. We could also see the confidence he
showed as he prepared to fight Goliath and the brain activity
involved in selecting just the right stones to achieve velocity and
accuracy to hit Goliath just below his helmet. There would be
no yips as he brought the sling back, just confidence based on
the brain waves created by his faith in God, which locks out
distractions, enabling focus. The brain activity involved would
be the same as someone about to shoot the game-winning shot,
although shooting a basketball never involves life-or-death
consequences.

All of these mind-altering events would have taken place in
David's mind, but they are also the types of brain activity that
each of us generate anytime the stakes are high in any endeavor.
That is why every great athlete who ever lived has been able to
focus his or her mind on the goal so great results will follow.

Many people have left a movie theater inspired by the movie
they saw, and many have changed their lives in dramatic ways.
Emotions are always the driving force behind this desired change
of direction as they help envision the dynamics of a better life.
Harnessing the mind's spiritual power and unleashing it in the
right direction should be the goal of every believer.

CHAPTER 9

Mind Control: Overcoming Addictions

If you were to drive around any large city in America, you would likely see several billboards for companies offering people help with addiction problems and how to bring their lives back from the brink of destruction. The one thing you will not see during this same drive around town is a billboard for companies offering help toward becoming addicted to various destructive behaviors. That is because no one needs help to become addicted; it just comes naturally. We are all addicts of any number of things, from drugs, cigarettes, and alcohol to texting, television, gambling, gossiping, playing video games, and shopping, just to name a few. For our own survival and by God's design, we are all addicted to the things that keep us alive. We are addicted to air, we are addicted to water, we are addicted to food, etc. If we try to do without them, our minds will pick up on this mutiny and ultimately force us to partake so we can live.

The question is not whether there are areas of our mind already locked out to run our machinery. The question is how much of the rest of our brain do we drown with substances and repetitive behaviors. The problem is God resides in our minds, every addictive sequence takes up valuable spiritual resources. That means that whatever brain cells are already used by these addictions, by definition, are not available for spiritual processing, locking God out of them since they are contrary to His nature.

It doesn't take a neuroscientist to understand that God can't exist in areas of the mind where addictions reside. If God were a person sitting up in the sky deciding everyone's fate by the luck of the draw, as many people think He does, then it wouldn't matter what we did to alter our brain's capabilities. Because God is Spirit and interacts with mankind solely in our minds, then it is imperative that we not saturate any more of our minds with ungodly things than humanly possible. There may be tens of millions of brain waves initially available for God's interaction to activate miracles and other incredible things in our lives and the lives of people around us. However, the more of them that are infected, the fewer that are accessible. Growing in faith increases the load capacity for God's Spirit in us; addictions kill it. It just means that faith in God is only possible in areas not already infected, while the cancer of addiction eats away at the remaining areas of the mind.

For today's generation of young people, the only time many of them try to become Bible scholars is when they are trying to justify drinking things the rest of the world drinks. They try to frame Jesus as a drinker and Timothy as a drinker just so they can try to find self-esteem in a can or bottle. Why would people purposely carpet bomb significant areas of their brains where God could reside with alcohol-related saturation? This diminishes any possible interaction with God in these areas, which, in effect, eliminates the possibility of extraordinary events in their lives.

Teenagers drinking anything addictive is like trying to build a fire while watering down the wood. They don't do it because they really think the Bible condones such irrational behavior. They do it because the drug of inclusion is perceived to be of far more value. It is bewildering that church leaders are so ineffective about influencing its members on this subject. Our goal should be to more closely resemble God and eliminate future crosses on the sides of the road. Although being religious requires little brain activity, being godly requires the mind to be hitting on all cylinders. God resides in the mind but doesn't occupy space in such a destructive neighborhood that drinking or any other biologically addictive behavior creates.

No miracle ever happens unless all of the participants' brain cells are focused on the goal and not dispersed by distractions. We can put all kinds of junk in our minds so they run as slowly as a virus-laden computer (which is a good analogy), or we can keep our minds renewed by drinking in as many godly virtues as possible. After all, God is already there in our minds through faith. Faith is a mental thing. Faith built the ark, and faith killed Goliath. Noah and David were just following the orders their minds through faith gave them. If we are only using about 10 percent of our brain's capabilities, there is plenty of room for God to set up shop.

The mind's destruction of faith-generating brain cells involves all addictive inputs. It pertains to smoking, drug addiction, sexual addiction, food addiction, as well as anything that chains us to our humanity. King David himself had a sexual addiction that ultimately led to his downfall. In the spring when kings go off to war, David didn't. The sun stays up longer when spring comes, making peeping at another's rooftop easier. David sent Uriah, Bathsheba's husband, off to war instead of leading him. Do we actually think this was David's first visual encounter with Bathsheba? The addictive nature of this event is evident by the fact that he had Uriah murdered so he could take Bathsheba as his wife while not considering its consequences. David spent nearly the whole year thereafter doing all of the rituals prescribed by Moses while never once having his conscience raise a flag about these incidents. Just like then, today sex is a drug that enslaves.

Of course, that is by God's own design. If it didn't enslave the mind, then replenishing the earth might not happen. However, just like any other biological temptation to do things that are against a person's best interest in the long run, one sexual encounter can alter a person's life forever. That is why there are instructions given in the operating manual about love, sex, and marriage that simply illustrate the best way to navigate around the necessary land mines of life that protect the treasure.

Warnings are given because the manufacturer knows how He made us. In the same way a car will have an operating manual that includes several sections with warnings about things to do and not to do, God's instructions about sex and other self-destructive, addictive temptations are simply warnings related to how we were made. It is true that obeying these warnings may take away some of the short-lived excitement of running off a cliff, but they will certainly prevent the resulting destruction and long-term consequences from such a foolish decision.

Basically, the Bible gives us a behind-the-scenes look at the

ring process, which we can ignore at our own peril. In
Jlysses had himself tied to the mast of his ship when
s' song was sung so he wouldn't be tempted by them.
Maybe ne should teach an Internet class for believers today.
Sex-related websites wouldn't thrive and distort the way human
sexuality was intended if there were no market for them. However,
putting our heads in the sand and ignoring their influence in our
culture minimizes its potential for destruction. Trying to sweep
our humanity under the rug and acting like we have nothing
addictive in our lives only ensures their continuation. The reason
we are to share our faults with one another is that no addict of
anything is able to diagnose himself.

Think of famous people whose illicit behavior became
known. Were they looking for intervention prior to its discovery?
Probably not. There is method in James's madness of instructing
believers to confess their faults to each other. Confessing sins
in the early stages of an addiction's development will kill the
addiction before it metastasizes and infects other parts of the
mind. It is obvious that when the Hebrew writer in the twelfth
chapter states that we should remove everything that hinders
and entangles us in the race of life, addictions would fall into
that category. As we all know, it is a lot easier to run without
weights attached to our ankles.

Since other people cannot see our thoughts, they can only
judge us by the things our bodies do. By the time some of
these thoughts become full blown, the resulting actions can
be irreversible. Lust and subsequent adultery would be a good
example. That is why divorces are so prevalent in the world and
in the church. The mind draws its inputs from the five senses—
taste, touch, smell, sight, and hearing—and then processes those

inputs, which then activates the body to execute the th
mind assigns the most value. We are not our bodies; we
minds.

Our spirits reside in our minds as well as our souls. Our
hopes and dreams and fears and everything else that comprises
who we are originate in the mind. Therefore, God shares
residence with everything else we fill our minds with, whether
it is work, family, friends, faith, lust, sports, or knowledge based
solely on our faith in Him or lack thereof.

We are able to keep our thoughts to ourselves, but what if we
couldn't? What if we had a ticker-tape scroll across our foreheads
noting every thought we had? Wouldn't that completely change
the way we think and the things we let go through our minds?
Actually, confessing our faults is not a suggestion; rather, it is
stated as a command. The treasure of God cannot be accessed
without sharing our minds with other believers because of its
diagnostic value. Confessing our faults stops errant thoughts
before they activate our bodies to do things that will blow up
in our faces.

It all comes down to control. If we don't control the things
our minds have to process, we can become involved in things
contrary to our best interests in the long run. Addictions and
spirituality are always mutually exclusive. Faith in God or
anything focused on long-term stasis is impossible when the
mind is consumed with solving its short-term problems with
addictive behavior. Miracles cannot originate in the mind in the
presence of addictions.

CHAPTER 10

Unleashing the Power of Perfection

"...stand firm. Let nothing move you. Always give yourself fully to the work of the Lord, because you know that your labor in the Lord is not in vain." (1 Cor. 15:58 NIV). Knute Rockne, a famous football coach, could not have said it better. Everyone wants to be a champion at something and every facet of life has its champions. Regardless of the activity, winners are those people who set goals and accomplish them; champions are those who set extraordinary goals and, against all odds, achieve them. Champions do unbelievable things and do not let others set the bar. They are typically just ordinary people inspired to do extraordinary things by some force within them; by some power or emotion or both that makes them want to move mountains. Champions are inspired to set these lofty goals by their investment toward the goal which helps set the trajectory toward it. People whose spirit is intertwined with God's Spirit are "inspired" to set extraordinary goals. Not ironically, that describes the entire list of special people of faith listed in Hebrews, chapters 11 & 12. Pick almost any hero in the Bible and for each of them, whenever someone tried to put boundaries around them, they were inspired by God to tear them down.

Practice Makes Perfect

Perfection. It's almost an offensive word, isn't it? Perhaps it's offensive because one of the things we can never be is perfect. But in this world, greatness typically comes from the realms of perfection, or rather, from its pursuit. Name any great musician or artist or athlete, and one of their primary attributes that separates them from everyone else in their field is their intense pursuit of perfection. Some of the greatest performances on any stage or athletic field have taken place when preparation and opportunity collided where that preparation was couched in the passion of trying to do something to perfection. After all, a person can't plan a miracle. However, extraordinary things tend to happen to people who put themselves in the right place at the right time, fueled by a passion to accomplish their goal. Although it is not about being a perfectionist, it is about setting the bar so high that even falling short could be well past everyone's expectations.

Just about everyone at some point in their lives, whether watching a sports show or television commercial, has seen Michael Jordan's game winning shot against the Cleveland Cavaliers in the 1989 NBA Eastern Conference playoffs. That play has been shown so much, the recording is probably worn out. With three seconds left on the clock and down by one point, Jordan worked hard to free himself to get the inbounds pass, and then dribbling to his left toward the free throw line, sank the game winning shot with Craig Ehlo trying to cover him. The thing that is most memorable about this shot is its aftermath. Since Ehlo had played a great game himself, having scored fifteen points in the fourth quarter and hitting a three point shot to put the Cavaliers ahead, he was understandably overwhelmed with emotion after seeing Jordan's shot go in, certainly realizing that his team's season was then over. While Ehlo laid on the floor measuring those emotions, Jordan was ecstatic from hitting the game winning. He celebrated with several fist pumps and then was mobbed by his teammates. It is an iconic moment that captured the emotions from both sides of the outcome as the camera painted the scene with a river of adrenalin.

Every kid who ever picked up a baseball has probably dreamed of driving in the winning run in a big game, and anyone who has ever put on a football uniform has probably imagined what it would be like to score the game winning touchdown. Likewise, anyone who has seen Michael Jordan hit that game winning shot has probably gone out the next day, with a basketball in his hands while facing the basketball goal in his driveway, and counted the seconds down to see if he could also hit that game winning shot. After all, winning is contagious.

The same applies to musicians, entertainers, actors and astronauts. People of all ages play their air guitars while listening to their favorite songs because they never learned to play the real thing. Karaoke probably evolved from the same reasoning. It is easy to daydream about performing a concert in front of thousands of people or playing a piano so beautifully that people in the audience stand and cheer. And what athlete hasn't imagined being carried off the playing field, court or diamond because of something great they did.

Many jobs and activities in life are emulated after seeing other people in those jobs do extraordinary things during extraordinary times. Whenever there is a major event or catastrophe where first responders go in and affect lives in a positive way, it often makes other people choose to pursue those same career paths. That is because it is ingrained in each of us to want to transition from the ordinary to the extraordinary. We would rather not just blend into the crowd; most people want their lives to matter. It may not even be about hitting the game winning shot. It may be about something far more important like trying to change the world so world hunger is eradicated or hundreds of other noble causes being achieved. Wishing any of these things to happen will not feed a single child or stop a single person from being abused. These things are not easily achieved, yet each of them can be accomplished simply by paying the price for making them happen.

Whatever name you choose to give it- pursuing perfection, pursuing excellence, giving it all you've got, giving 110%, or perhaps the one with the highest calling: holiness- each of them say the same thing, just in a different context. Each involves an emotional component that erases the upper boundaries of possibility. Impossible things are most likely to happen when things seem their bleakest in either arena. It may be difficult for us to equate an athlete who collapses in victory after overcoming seemingly impossible odds with a servant of God also laying everything on the line, but many of the stories written in the Bible illustrate exactly that. What athlete can say they fought a giant in a battle to the death against odds so great that nobody gave David any hope of victory? And what entertainer has ever stood before a crowd so hostile that the audience wanted to tear him limb from limb like the Apostle Paul faced many times because of the things he said, hoping to inspire them to achieve greatness themselves?

As we know, there is an enormous difference between the excellence an athlete or entertainer pursues and that of a follower of Christ. Athletes and entertainers typically only need a small set of skills to become great in their arena while Christians are called upon to leave no stone unturned to eliminate weaknesses while working on strengths. In fact, that is what defines us. To become great in their field of work, athletes and entertainers typically don't work on life skills that might adversely affect their lives. In the world, highlighting a person's strengths while sweeping their weaknesses under the rug is one way to get noticed, if only for a short while. Unfortunately, it seems there are news stories about these stars just about every day who forgot to address their weaknesses which ultimately lead to their downfall. They buy into the world whispering how great they are. Since as Christians our training reinforces the power of being a servant, we shouldn't be as tempted to think we are the source of our success.

That is why the apostle Paul had the Corinthians focus on their weaknesses as a means to an end by showing them how to excel while protecting against the things that might bring them down. Some stars would have better lives today if they had heeded that advice. Paul reminded the Corinthians of his religious pedigree as he told them the story of him asking God to remove his thorn in the flesh three times to no avail. Have you ever thought about what thorn he was referring to? Well, Paul could have been thinking of something else, but one "thorn" he had to continually deal with was his sight problems. There were several illustrations where Paul's sight apparently was limited. First of all, Tertius penned many of his letters instead of Paul doing it himself (Romans 16:22). Secondly, when Paul stood before the Sanhedrin to defend himself, he couldn't tell that his accuser was the high priest (Acts 23:5). In the pomp of the

position, anyone, even with limited sight, could tell wh
priest was. Thirdly, Paul noted in the letters he person
that he used large letters (Galatians 6:11). We take fc
that vision centers are everywhere in our culture but back in the
first century, there were none. Imagine people today without
corrective lens or surgery.

Whatever biologically happened to Paul when he was
blinded by the light on the road to Damascus may have created
long-term sight issues for him. By asking God to remove his
metaphoric thorn in the flesh, it was as if Paul was telling God
how much stronger and more effective an orator he would be
or how many more people he could win over if his physical
limitation was corrected. Instead, as Paul related the story,
God reminded him that a person's strengths glorify themselves
while working within the boundaries of weaknesses can only
glorify God. As Paul quoted this reminder: "...my power is
made perfect in weakness." (2 Cor. 12:9 NIV). That is not to
say that weakness creates perfection, but someone who commits
their entire being toward overcoming their weaknesses will only
do so to glorify God rather than themselves.

Pursuing a perfect life—a godly life—with all our hearts,
souls, minds, and strength will make unbelievable things happen
simply by the emotions and focus involved in that pursuit. That
is exactly how elite athletes approach their chosen work, and it
should be the same for people of faith. Although a ball game is
played between the lines, it is what happens outside the lines
when nobody is looking that defines what takes place inside
those lines. There is a reason our coaches made us do all those
drills during practice. They made us do them because repetition
creates perfection. Our inspiration to excel may have been the

fear of having to run sprints if we didn't do it right or getting to go in early if we did, but eventually attributes were acquired to help us succeed.

In the same way, while the game of life is played between the lines for everyone to see, it is the things we do when nobody is looking that predicates how powerful God can be in our lives. Nobody sitting on the bench ever hit a game winning shot so the most important aspect of Jesus' teachings is to strive for excellence and His spirit within us will do the rest.

CHAPTER 11

Transforming the Roles of Men and Women in the Church

Serve and Volley

It's been a long time since I have played mixed doubles in tennis, but from the mixed doubles I've seen on television, the strategy for victory hasn't really changed: hit the ball at the girl. Success is then determined by whichever team can best counterbalance their weaknesses with their strengths. Appropriately, both members of the winning team will equally share the prize, even though their talents and contributions may differ. Men and women are certainly different, but when they are on the same team, they are equal. Men may physically be much stronger than women, and this, throughout history, has affected the safety and security of women and families in all cultures. However, God's nature is best quantified when both men's and women's attributes are considered.

God created men and women as spiritual equals—teammates, soul mates, partners, and equals. But just as women were second-class citizens in various cultures and societies throughout the ages, they were also second-class citizens in the church in the first century. This has continued through the present time. It has just been in the last ninety years in America that women were *given* the right to vote by men, and the words of the apostle Peter still reverberate in the church today that wives are to be submissive to their husbands (1 Peter 3:1). These words have been the source of low self-esteem for women as some men have used them as their authority to control their wives. It doesn't mean men are supposed to utilize or interpret Scripture this way, but it has certainly happened to the detriment and reputation of the church. If women are struggling to find their spiritual identity because of the words of Paul or Peter concerning their place on the team, it is because of the interpretation and not the intent of the words themselves.

God's Word should be the source of strength and self-esteem for His people instead of a component for its absence. It is essential, then, that Scripture is interpreted in its context to accomplish that goal. For example, the only way to glean wisdom from Paul's letter to the Ephesians is to go sit in one of the house churches in Ephesus and experience their way of life before bringing those words forward into today's world.

Paul instructed the women in Ephesus, Corinth, and Colosse that they were to be submissive to their husbands, while Peter reiterated these instructions to women in a similar region. Do those instructions apply today? Should women still be second-class citizens in the church? Why or why not? When you think about it, having one-half of an organization being submissive to the other half is not a good foundation for that organization to flourish or to keep the submissive half of its members.

Paul wrote some of his instructions about women being submissive to their husbands during his first imprisonment in

THIS APPEARS TO ASSUME THAT PETER WAS SAYING THAT WOMEN ARE 2ND CLASS CITIZENS.

Rome. There appears to be three congregational letters that he wrote during this imprisonment: Ephesians and Colossians, which were churches in Asia Minor, as well as Philippians, whose congregation was located in Europe. Although Paul never mentioned anything about submission to the church at Philippi (where he stayed at the house of Lydia and worked side by side with other women for the gospel), he made it a focus in his letters to Asia Minor. Why is that? Perhaps it is because Asia Minor (Ephesus) was home to the Temple of Artemis, which fostered an atmosphere of women's rights as well as being the center of slave trading in the Roman Empire. As Acts 19 notes, there was a passion in Ephesus concerning the Temple of Artemis (Diana), and the Ephesians didn't want anyone messing with her or the income derived from her.

Paul incorporated a format for Christian submission in his letters. 1) Men were supposed to be submissive to authorities; 2) women were supposed to be submissive to their husbands; and 3) slaves were supposed to be submissive to their masters. Paul stated in his letters that women were to be submissive to their husbands as the church was to be submissive to Christ, and Peter echoed these instructions in 1 Peter. It is erroneous to equate this scenario with modern events because girls in ancient times were given in marriage as early as twelve or thirteen years old to men they did not choose but were chosen for them. Of course, they needed to submit to their husband for their own well-being. As such, these were appropriate words for these Gentile churches trying to be a light in the community. In many cultures, women and girls were considered a man's property. First, they were the property of their fathers and then, when they married, they became the property of their husbands.

In other cultures, women had extremely limited rights and privileges. I think you would find it an interesting exercise to study women's existence in each culture of the world at that time and the instructions given to the churches in that particular area. This was not done as punishment; it was done for their protection and survival. Women weren't strong enough to fend for themselves in those times and in those countries, so it was important that they did what they were told to do, just like slaves were to do what they were told to do.

Husbands had accepted responsibility for their wives' welfare, so women needed to follow their husbands' lead. Note that Paul was careful to instruct husbands to always love their wives while he never once instructed women to love their husbands. Shouldn't that raise a red flag about our interpretation of Scripture? The paradox of Paul's words noting that men were to love their wives while the bar Paul set for their wives only included being respectful to their husbands (Eph. 5:33 NIV), should signal cultural differences between then and now. These words would fit a situation where someone was assigned the person they were to marry. In Paul's letter to Titus, Paul instructed him to have the older women teach the younger women to love their husbands. By definition of his instructions, they didn't love their husbands when they married. How could they?

Obviously, it must have been an issue or Paul and Peter would not have had to address it. They both equated submission of wives and slaves the same. In fact, Peter used this exact language. It should send chills up our spines when he says in 1 Peter 3:1 that wives should be submissive to their husbands "in the same way" slaves are to be submissive to their masters. This line of thinking obviously didn't work because we read in

CHRIST WAS USED AS THE EXAMPLE OF SUBMISSION IN EARLIER SCRIPTURE, NOT JUST SLAVES & WIVES.

104

1 Timothy 2:11 where Paul, a few years later, tried to fix the problem in Ephesus. He pulled out all stops in his letter to Timothy by referring to Adam's and Eve's garden adventure, going back to his Jewish roots. Even though Adam also sinned by eating the fruit, Paul tried to influence these Gentile women by noting it was Eve who sinned first, so therefore, women should be submissive to their husbands.

I can't imagine this strategy worked either since Gentile women would not likely be influenced by the Jewish story of creation. Paul even flipped the argument in his letter to the church at Rome that he was trying to impress, by stating that it was the sin by Adam (rather than Eve) that started the ball rolling in the wrong direction. Paul had already tried beating the Corinthian women over the head (figuratively speaking) by noting that the Law said they must be in submission (1 Cor. 14:34 NIV), but based on Paul's frustration in 2 Corinthians, that Jewish approach didn't work on this Gentile audience either. Being a Roman citizen may have given him access to these Gentile cities, but that would not necessarily have generated enough influence to induce those Gentiles to follow Jewish customs.

Voting Rights

Today, women are no longer property so those synergies no longer exist. Just because Paul and Peter penned words for their audience in the first century does not mean those words are relevant today, especially since they run counter to the nature of God. The authors' ancient points about women submitting to men are therefore irrelevant because those metaphors died an appropriate death. Well, actually they are not irrelevant. It is just that men and women should submit to each other equally as their talents and strengths dictate, as equal members of the same team. So the missing part of the equation is men learning to be submissive to women in the same way women are to be submissive to men. To be able to do that, men would have to first submit their will to Christ which would then take care of the rest.

Submission is a very important part of teamwork in any context. However, it seems in the church it is the way the word *submission* has been defined that has created the erroneous juxtaposition among its teammates. Submission, as Jesus defined it is simply putting the will of others before our own. Athletics provide a good backdrop of how this should play out between teammates and ultimately between men and women. For example, no matter how great a basketball player Lebron James is, he still must put the will of his teammates before his own as part of a team. After all, that is what being part of a team is all about. However, being in submission to the will of the team still means that Lebron should take over the last five minutes of a game and do anything else his talents create to win. Yes, that is submission. It is imperative the church learns the same lesson. Submission is about using one's gifts in the best interest of others; it should never be about burying one's talents just to keep peace in the family or in the church. The lesson men have to learn is that dying to one's self involves burying all of the stereotypical characteristics of men that our culture has created and then living like Christ. A man should use his talents as a beacon through which his wife's talents can shine, and vice versa so the light they create together shines far brighter than anything they could do on their own.

Sometimes a person has to take a bullet for the team, metaphorically speaking. Paul actually told the men on the Ephesian team they should submit to one another out of reverence to Christ. This is a great team strategy. Even though his next sentence told women they were to submit to their husbands (Eph. 5:21–22), we should remember they were never unequal in God's sight, nor are they now. They are on the same team, just with different attributes. I would think that had there been a woman in the upper room, Jesus would have washed her feet as well. After all, it's all about the team.

So let's stop here and explain to our college student who is evaluating whether she wants to continue in the church, what you believe about men's and women's roles in the church. If Jesus had come during our generation, would Peter and Paul have written the same instructions about women as they did in the first century? What will the church look like ten thousand years from now related to the roles of women? Should women start their own church to get away from men's teachings about the Bible? If women's strengths were interlocked with men's strengths as equals, how would the church be different than it is now?

Let's see if we can put this into some perspective. Men have been in charge of the church since its inception even though Jesus never taught that they should be. During that time, men decided the church should go to war, ultimately initiating the Crusades. It was men who decided that women should be burned at the stake, thinking them to be witches hundreds of years ago. People today note that the church was misguided about grace in the 1950s and 1960s, but it wasn't the church that was misguided about grace; it was the men leading the church who had it all wrong. Do we think that women would have ever had a problem with grace? In past decades, men in charge of the church could not even tell their own children they loved them even though God continually told His own Son He loved Him.

Leading By Example

Had women been in charge of the church when the current exodus of youth began to proliferate, they would have sought help in resolving its problems. They would have done anything necessary to help young people find faith, just as they typically are the ones who will get out of the car to ask someone for directions. Realizing that many times a woman's attributes can promote more productivity than an alpha male's attributes can, corporations are handing over the reins to women with greater frequency. The church should do the same, especially in areas of God's nature where a woman is stronger. When the church excludes the leadership gifts of women, it is operating short-handed.

If Jesus were in charge of a company, his management style would resemble women's attributes more than it would men's attributes. It would be nurturing, it would be empathetic, it would be inspirational and it would focus on people's lives. Come to think about it, Jesus is in charge of the church so those characteristics should emanate from any people leading His church. Since the first century, the church has been operated as a top down religion by the men who decided it should be run that way. Scripture does not support that belief.

On the other hand, thinking that women could lead the church in its current setup is just as erroneous as thinking that men can lead. Although women have many great attributes, they also have weaknesses which would adversely affect the church as much as the way men's weaknesses are now affecting the church. Common sense tells us that no set gender or group should actually be in charge of the other. Interweaving the strengths of both men and women into the fabric of the church while addressing their weaknesses through the use of Jesus' teachings will attract a wide range of people to it.

The lesson men should learn is that leadership is not a right bestowed on anyone. Like respect, it must be earned by demonstrating effective leadership in the same way Jesus led his disciples. Considering the attributes of God and His Son, the person who has them in abundance should show everyone else how they acquired them regardless of gender.

So does that mean women should be allowed to become leaders in the church or part of the church hierarchy? No, because there should not be a hierarchy in the church in the first place. Whose idea was it to create a hierarchy? It certainly wasn't Jesus' idea or teaching. In fact, when His disciples asked Him what the pecking order would be in His kingdom, He taught them a lesson of service and submission, ending the conversation. There is no pecking order, just a need to serve each other equally. Jesus basically taught about what each of us needs to do to tap into God's power and avoid life's land mines. Adding a layer of structure to the simple way of life He taught about is counterproductive. Of course, that didn't keep the apostles from doing it anyway.

The apostles were great and godly men, intent on following in Jesus' footsteps. However, they were not flawless by any stretch of the imagination. As the Sanhedrin noted, these were ordinary men doing extraordinary things because of Jesus' influence in their lives (Acts 4:13 NIV) while the Holy Spirit coming upon them during this period of authentication strengthened their resolve. That did not mean they didn't struggle with the things being thrown at them. Paul struggled with the church at Corinth even though he had worked with them for eighteen months (Acts 18:11 NIV) and the Holy Spirit had given them miraculous powers. When Jesus was alive, each of the apostles wanted to be in charge, evidenced by some of them wondering out loud who would be the greatest in the kingdom. After His ascension, instead of going into all the world and preaching the gospel, they hunkered down in Jerusalem to manage the church. Unfortunately, that wasn't their mission. The sole purpose of Jesus having apostles was for them to be His witnesses to the ends of the earth. In effect, they were to be photo journalists who could tell stories about what they heard and saw with vivid, high definition clarity (what fishermen can't tell stories?). Being twelve apostles, they would be able to chronicle Jesus' life and death from twelve different camera angles. Since fishermen and tax collectors are typically detail-oriented, they would be able to supply details that other occupations might miss.

Had it been Jesus, upon learning that the Grecian widows weren't being cared for, He would have personally gone to each of them and touched their lives. The apostles sent other people. When Paul and Barnabas returned from their first missionary journey and problems arose that needed to be addressed, the apostles could have used this opportunity to go into the world and preach the gospel by going with Paul and Barnabas to Antioch. Instead, they sent other people. And thirty years after Jesus' death, the apostles were bragging to Paul after he returned from his third missionary journey about how they had continued to follow the Jewish Law and its practices. They then threw Paul under the bus by making him adhere to these Jewish customs, ultimately getting him arrested. To make matters worse, there is no evidence they came to his rescue.

Here are some questions to consider while searching for the lost faith of youth in this jungle the world created:

+ Was everything out of the mouths of the apostles infallible?
+ Why did Paul tell the Thessalonians that Jesus would return in his lifetime?
+ When Paul called Peter on the carpet for his hypocrisy at the church in Antioch, it is possible there were other instances where Peter or any of the other apostles erred, including their writings?
+ Did they overstep their authority when they chose to run the church in Jerusalem instead of going into all of the world?
+ Had they preached the gospel to the ends of the earth as instructed, would Paul's calling have been necessary?
+ Did Jesus know that forty years from the time of His ascension that Rome would destroy Jerusalem, making the gospel's export so urgent that someone who had persecuted Jesus had to be called to do the apostles' job?
+ Why did Christianity become a sect within Judaism?

Now you can see how the world is bombarding young people. How would you answer each of these questions for them?

Leaders are people others choose to follow. Paul wasn't selecting leaders in any church; he was identifying them. Whenever a basketball team selects someone to be their captain, it will always be somebody they are already following based on that person's ability to lead and inspire people to follow in their footsteps. It should be noted that sometimes Paul appointed leaders and sometimes he did not. It certainly wasn't a theological requirement. In fact, while in Corinth writing to the Thessalonians or in Ephesus writing to the Corinthians, Paul never appointed leaders of the churches in these particular groups. Paul mistakenly taught that Jesus was coming back in his lifetime just as Peter did, and because of that, there was no urgency to appoint anyone to lead.

The attributes of each member of any particular team dictate their roles on that team, and the church should be no exception. The roles of each man and woman in a congregation should be related to their strengths and weaknesses. Typically, men have certain strengths and weaknesses while women have other strengths and weaknesses. The same should be true in the church regarding spiritual qualities. If a man is leading an area of spiritual growth and a woman in the group could inspire others to be more godly, then, by definition, they aren't growing as they could with a different quarterback.

People mistakenly think that Paul provided Timothy and Titus with qualifications for selecting leaders in the church in his letters to them. First of all, they are not called *qualifications* and should not be considered as such. The characteristics that Paul included in either list are, at best, prerequisites rather than a synopsis of what a leader in the church should look like. Secondly, Timothy and Titus had been with Paul for years so they would have been well aware of what constituted leadership characteristics. Paul was just giving them some food for thought as these Jewish young men assisted these Gentile congregations.

Thirdly, we know Paul's lists are not actually qualifications for leaders of the church because neither Paul, John the Baptist, nor Jesus Himself would be qualified to lead based on the things Paul wrote to Timothy and Titus.

There is only one qualification for anyone leading in any area of the church: resembling Christ in as many attributes as possible while confessing and actively working on their weaknesses. A leader is someone who can confidently tell others the path they have walked for a life filled with love, joy and peace as well as providing the directions to the treasure.

Women should not just be given a larger role in operating the church in the flawed model men set up centuries ago. Women should have an equal role in deciding what the church model should look like and how best to use the talents of everyone in the church to lift each other up. There is a good chance the format of the church that women and men working together with a clean sheet of paper would create might be significantly different than the format men created long ago. Regardless of the results of that effort, it should be at the forefront of everyone in the church that the current model isn't working and, therefore, must be changed so faith can thrive.

Let's forget all of the theological baggage that has thrown the church off track and focus on what will make us stronger in the Lord. Just watch the people who are exemplifying Christ who you would like to emulate, and follow their example, whether men or women. An *example* is the only thing that should be followed. If someone is hung up on titles or gender, then this way of life is probably not for him or her anyway. All people should lead in the things they are strong in and follow in the things they are not as we help each other become more like Christ.

CHAPTER 12

Building a Spiritual Fitness Center

For insomniacs or early risers, most of the availability of television programs is limited. Before the sun comes up, infomercials typically rule the airwaves, enticing you to try this or buy that. As one flips through the channels during these late-night or early-morning hours, it doesn't take long to find one of those thirty-minute advertisements about exercise equipment, weight-loss supplements, or other self-help angles. Their main selling point seems to be that if you are not satisfied with yourself (and who is?), then by buying this particular product, your problems will be solved. These advertisements typically show some pictures of people before they tried their product and then show pictures of those same people after they have reportedly used the product. Obviously, for effect, the pictures of the same person are extremely different.

The "before" pictures typically show an unsmiling, unhappy, and overweight person dressed in frumpy clothes with bird's-nest hair while the "after" pictures typically represent a happy, smiling, trim, and well-groomed person who is ready to take on the world. A credit card number is all it takes to live an "after" life.

Although there may be some question as to the effectiveness of these types of products, it does present the question about the before and after pictures of someone engaged in the Christian life. The photographs of any of us may or may not change as we grow in Spirit and love, but what do the spiritual before and after pictures look like? When we grow in Spirit, what changes? When we grow in love, will anyone notice the difference? How can we shed thirty pounds of spiritual flab so the after effect will make someone else want to buy the product we are selling? Just because a person wants to grow in love or lose thirty pounds does not mean it will automatically happen.

Marathon Training

As you drive down any highway, you may see various bumper stickers on the backs of cars. Some of them are inspirational while others are, well, not so much. It may be true that a picture is worth a thousand words, but there are two particular bumper stickers that seem to be far more informative than that. These two bumper stickers create an emotional connection for those who pay the price to earn them as well as admiration from those who understand their meaning. Those two inspirational bumper stickers are "13.1" and "26.2."

These bumper stickers are actually much smaller than usual bumper stickers, but they say so much more. For anyone who might not know their relevance, they represent people who run marathons and half marathons. Just like the marathons in ancient Greece, marathons today are 26.2 miles in length while half marathons are 13.1 miles long. These small pieces of paper stuck on bumpers and rear windows relate the commitment of time and energy of the runner as well as their family toward this pursuit. It tells an incredible story about the training the runners go through day after day after day to create the endurance to run that distance. It demonstrates the perseverance and self-control of the runner who must endure the conditions and distractions as well as the pounding his or her body would take to reach a place in his or her life to finish such a race.

It also highlights the attributes such an athlete would need: focus, passion, endurance, patience, strength, commitment, and many more of equal weight. For what it is worth, these are also the exact same attributes of someone passionately pursuing spiritual training. It may be paradoxical, but strengthening the body while increasing one's physical endurance begins with a spiritual commitment while strengthening one's mind while increasing spiritual endurance, begins with a physical commitment. Ultimately, these elite athletes push the limits to maximize their emotional strength (heart), spiritual strength (soul), physical strength (strength), and mental endurance (mind) which helps them succeed. This was the power Moses was trying to get the children of Israel to learn to harness.

Training is involved in all disciplines, whether playing a sport, driving a car, helping your neighbor, or learning to love God, other people, and even ourselves. In the upper room, when Jesus commanded His disciples to love one another, I'm sure they would like to have had an instruction manual telling them exactly how to do that since they had previously been fighting over who would be the greatest in the coming kingdom. Although they were followers of Jesus, they were also rivals for His attention.

As a training exercise, Jesus demonstrated the full extent of His love by washing His disciples' feet to paint a picture for them of what love looked like. By commanding them to love one another, He wasn't expecting them to be instantly filled with love for each other any more than a couch potato can be commanded to run a marathon. Growing in God's nature is a process, just like growing in anything else. Whether one is a marathoner, a swimmer, a sprinter, or any other Olympic-type athlete, there are specific exercises designed to strengthen specific areas of the body to make the whole body stronger. For example, lifting weights might be useful for building strong biceps and triceps, while aerobic exercises might be useful for strengthening obliques and cardiovascular endurance.

Any athlete knows the importance of working on those muscles that are the weakest rather than focusing on those that are the strongest to balance the whole. That is because athletes know it is their weaknesses that will beat them. A person might be the fastest person on earth for the first fifty yards of a race, but if the race is one hundred yards long, then it may be the person's endurance level that beats him or her rather than his or her lack of speed.

Strengthening the Church

Imagine that a particular church had several of its members suffer heart attacks in the space of a few weeks, prompting action by its leaders. The leaders decided that in the best interest of its members, they would tear out everything inside the church building and install exercise equipment. In the sanctuary and auditorium, they took out all the pews and installed treadmills in their place. In the area where the baptistry and choir loft stood, recumbent bicycles and weight-lifting equipment were positioned. Around the perimeter of the auditorium, a walking and jogging track was installed, and where the pulpit and communion tables once were, aerobics and yoga classes were now held.

Because members saw how poor health affected other members, they all bought into the changes. Members were now encouraging other members in their efforts to eat a healthy diet, get proper exercise, and lift whatever weights they could to increase bone density. They might not have been doing any religious rituals like they did before, but they were communing together toward a common goal.

The community heard about what was going on at that local church, and many of their neighbors started coming to the church to exercise with them because of the value it presented. While they would have never darkened the doors of that church to be part of a religious exercise, they came to be part of the church to become physically stronger. Their health care costs came down as they became healthier, and they formed closer bonds with each other. Endorphins were now rocking this church as the fellowship and focus they shared fed their need to be a part of something bigger than themselves. Whenever someone missed a workout, one of his partners would call him to be sure he was okay, as they had become one with each other.

By the way, in this newly configured congregation, the people who led each of the activities were the ones most qualified to lead those activities. With the focus of the group so clear, there was no gender differentiation among the group. Men are better leaders when it comes to lifting weights, so one of them led that activity even though women were part of that group; women are better leaders of the yoga and aerobics classes, so they led those classes even though men were part of that group. Although it is important that there is some structure to ensure the most efficient path toward a goal, there was no need for hierarchy in this community. The best leaders led.

This is just an imaginary story, but the underlying theme about the need for spiritual fitness is real. The church was never intended to be part of a religion or a religion in and of itself; it was intended solely to be a spiritual fitness center, with Jesus as its leader. He was versed on all of the spiritual equipment we would need for strength of faith and showed us how to use it. In the religion of Christianity, young people are leaving the church because all they see are spiritually flabby people sitting in the pews chained to their religion. They see spiritual couch potatoes giving instructions about how to run a marathon, and they aren't buying it.

Instead of an imaginary story about a church that empties out its auditorium and sanctuary to install fitness equipment, let's envision a congregation of people intent on growing spiritually strong. Envision a congregation of people who have installed the best spiritual fitness equipment ordered through God's Word, since it is already paid for. Since God is spiritual strength, we would start by identifying God's attributes and then working backward. God has hundreds of incredible characteristics that we should emulate. Just like any discipline, there are specific practices and drills we can do to help create them.

In your Bible study classes or on your own, take the time to list as many of God's attributes as you can that will promote spiritual growth. For me, the most important attribute of God that makes everything else on the list doable is focus. Each of these attributes have their own exercises and drills to foster strength, but just like any discipline, such as trying to lose weight, without focus to overcome the mind's objections, nothing exceptional will ever occur. The first attribute of God to emulate through drills should be focus.

The goal is to retrain the mind so it uses areas of the brain where God resides with better clarity. From there, it is easier to experience God. Instead of doing the religious rituals churches currently do that destroy faith in adults and young people, perhaps we should do spiritual drills designed to address specific spiritual problems, such as strengthening the mind, which God occupies. There are enumerable drills that could broaden the mind's capabilities in godly directions. One of them might include focusing attention on a given number of people each week through notes or conversations and increasing that number as the mind grows in God's nature. Another way could simply be by memorizing scripture. No matter which methods are used to increase mental firepower, the end result should be something that shows the family resemblance between us and God.

CHAPTER 13

Worshipping an Omniscient God

People typically think of going to worship whenever they think of going to church even though they are basically exact opposites. That is because "going to church" is about going somewhere to be with other people who believe as you do, while valuating God is an individual assessment. Worship is not something a person does; worship is simply the value we assign to God.

The worship service of the church that many of us have attended most of our lives is supposed to be a demonstration of what God is worth to us. You know, "worthship," which is where the word *worship* comes from. For as far back in time as anyone can remember, people have assembled to worship God, which I guess by definition is their way of informing God what He means to them. The problem with doing that, in and of itself, is that it actually defines God as not being omniscient. In fact, no matter what denomination of the church a particular congregation is or what events occur in their worship service, everything that is done in any worship service pigeon-holes God as requiring maintenance.

In the Christian religion of about two billion people, just

about everyone gives lip service to the fact that God is omniscient, but every action we as believers perform is to the contrary. If you were to ask believers why they sing songs of praise to God, they would likely tell you that it was so God would know how much they love and worship Him. If you were to ask them why they said prayers to God, they would likely say it was so God would know what they need and understand the depth of their faith. If you were to ask them why they took the Lord's Supper, they would likely say that it was so they could commune with Jesus. All of this is well and good, but doing these things for those reasons only reinforces the idea that God doesn't know without us telling Him.

This is why there needs to be a dynamic change in the way the church functions when it comes together as a band of believers. If the church actually heard itself say out loud why we do the things we do in the worship service, then the problem would probably fix itself. Is it any wonder that kids are confused about the things we have been teaching them? Here's a challenge: go to any high school class in any church and ask the teenagers why they do the things they do in the worship service. There is a great likelihood they will not have a clue why. It is a reminder that we have to unlearn what we think we know about the church before laying out a better way of becoming more like God.

Let's start this whole process all over again. Mentally, take yourself to a place where there are no rituals of any kind. There are no leaders, nor are there any pews or steeples setting on top of the church buildings because there are no church buildings either. Imagine that it is just you, all by yourself, trying to strengthen your faith in God so you can tap into God's power. It doesn't matter if you are a boy or girl, man or woman, young or old. There is one agenda and one agenda only: finding God's riches. There's only one problem—you don't know where they are. That is because you only have a small piece of the treasure map and a limited understanding of God. Everyone else only has their own small piece of the map as well. You have certain skills useful for finding the treasure, but you also have certain weaknesses and shortcomings that preclude it from ever being found. For example, you might be the best digger in the world, but if your directional skills were lacking, then you would always be digging in the wrong place.

The obvious answer to this enigma is for everyone to come together and combine their pieces of the treasure map to show the intended path to the treasure. That would be like several people hunting for the same treasure, yet pooling their resources to increase the likelihood of its discovery. That is why everything we do in the religion of Christianity should be to promote the pursuit of perfection, not to see how many rituals we can perform. As such, anything that is done solely because we think we are supposed to, becomes a meaningless ritual that should jettisoned. In fact, there should not be a single ritual used by the church at any time if it doesn't promote an emotional connection between believers.

How do we know what is a meaningless ritual and what is not? If someone can daydream, text, pass notes or sleep during an activity, then it is a ritual and should be eliminated. Rituals should not be involved in any part of our time together because they block the emotional connection between participants. We should spend our time together honing our skills while confessing our weaknesses rather than just going through the motions.

A disciple of Christ is someone intent on mastering the discipline of Christ, no matter how impossible it is. That is what defines a disciple, while the intensity of that pursuit dictates its boundaries. The drills and exercises toward that pursuit should be those that educate, inspire or encourage during our time together. We should read our Bibles to help understand the God we are trying to be like so we can anticipate the clues leading to His nature. Then we can be certain we are heading in the right direction. Just like a football coach who inspires his team to lay it all on the field of battle during his halftime talk, our time together should provide the inspiration for the coming week. It should demonstrate the power of God to everyone we meet. If they see exponential love, joy, peace and patience in our lives, they will want to know how to have it themselves. Everything we do during our time together should provide the encouragement to help us stay the course when times get tough.

The reality is that worshipping God is not an event. A "physical" worship service may only be an hour or two in length but the "spiritual" worship service for an omniscient being is 168 hours long each week, with no beginning and no end. We should come together as a team of believers to push each other toward becoming more like God. Thinking that any words out of our mouths would declare to God what He is worth defines our misinterpretation of Scripture. The things we do the other 167 hours define what God is worth to us when nobody is looking.

When families exchange Christmas gifts with each other, they typically buy something for somebody that many times is something they would actually like to have themselves. The worship service was originally set up to be a novel way of exchanging gifts with each other. The way it was intended, believers would come together to share gifts while not actually having to give up the things that are shared. Wouldn't that be a cool way to do Christmas! In this spiritual gift exchange, the amount we receive is directly related to the amount we try to give away. That defines what synergy among believers should look like.

Let's see what changes should be made in our time together that might help facilitate learning more about God.

Prayer

Just like the worship service, communicating with God is not an event in that it has no beginning or end. We might say, "Amen" at the end of the prayer, but we are still communicating with God. Anyone who has ever owned a cell phone has probably thought he either hung it up but didn't or has accidentally called someone by mistake. In either case, someone on the other end of the line has access to your words through this open mike without your knowledge. Communicating with God is like living with our microphones stuck in the open position. Prayer is a focus drill of things that are important to those praying.

All of this begs the question: what are we to expect from our prayers? As James noted about Elijah, "The effectual fervent prayer of a righteous man avails much" (James 5:16 KJV). This is very true. That is because of the focus involved in that fervor where the entire brain's activities are rowing the boat in the same direction. The power of prayer is solely in the spiritual focus it creates. Directing all of our mental firepower onto a given person or situation can create a chain reaction so powerful that God's Spirit working in us can create miracles. Anytime distractions are eliminated by the powerful emotions associated with prayer, incredible things can happen. Although it is way too easy for a group prayer to become a meaningless ritual, by learning to channel our full attention onto the brain cells the Creator of the universe occupies in our minds, there is no limit to the size of the snowball that can be created.

Prayer is a waste of time if it focuses attention on things that run counter to the nature of God living within us. For example, a person praying to God that he not get lung cancer while still puffing on cigarettes or praying for clean arteries while eating junk food illustrates divergent priorities. None of us should expect intervention in any situation where the request belittles God's nature. A person belittles God when he drives home intoxicated but asks for God to keep him from killing someone.

In prayer, people tend to give God a list of things to do while not assigning God's Spirit in them that task. God does not run a Jehovah's Repair Service truck around town to handle the list of things we would like Him to do so any requested interaction must first come from a commitment of one's own time and energy. It is also fruitless to place a window of time on any request, which means petitioning God's intervention in people's lives should begin five, ten, and even twenty years before any problems might arise. If someone has a family history of a given illness, then praying about it twenty years in advance to help educate and strengthen resolve would be godly intervention.

The sole purpose of communicating with God is to initiate an emotional avalanche. Whenever we pray to God, whether in public or private, it is the focus we place on the issues causing us to stop the flow of life long enough for hearts and hands to be joined together. Praying to an omniscient God should never be an intellectual exercise or ritual with predictable phrases, requests, or expectations where we tell God what He needs to do for us. Avalanches are never predictable. Prayer is about creating an emotional connection between each member participating, like joining batteries together in series where spiritual power flows from person to person, empowering those in need. The intent of prayer is to train the mind to continually lay everything on the line to maintain that emotional connection because God does not reside in comfort zones.

Understanding whether a requesting prayer works begins with the biology of faith in the mind, where God's Spirit resides in believers. It is impossible for God to not grant every spiritual request. That is, we have full control over whether we increase in, say, patience or joy based on how God's Spirit works in us. Accomplishing this only requires focusing on those desired things. Faith in God allows God access to our inner being, with the mind controlling our thoughts and actions. The amount of control is directly related to the activities associated with it. We can pray for these things if that helps us get our arms around the nature of God by personifying Him, but ultimately the desire for spiritual things that embody God's nature are there for the taking, with the only limitation being our faith or lack thereof.

One way to increase the amount of the 168 hours each week that we are acutely aware of our communication with God is to note the time spent in this mental communication. This will make it a whole lot easier to stay focused on godly things. Our minds constantly process information in one form or another, so the more of that time spent considering God, the less time there will be for the mind to wander into areas leading away from the treasure. Although prayer is just a focus drill, it is one of the most important tools for growing in God's nature because, if done correctly and with the proper non-religious intent, it can expand our ability to feel each other's pain and triumphs. Are we to pray without ceasing? Absolutely, because communicating with an omniscient God never ends.

Singing Songs of Praise

The sole purpose of singing songs during our time together is to channel the river of emotion that faith in God creates so that it flows in the same direction. Contrary to what is taught in Christianity, we are not actually singing to God because God reads hearts rather than music. Singing words instead of reading words opens the adrenal glands to promote God's penetration into areas of the mind reserved for cautious behavior. Singing alters the mind as long as there is focus involved in its execution. If all we are doing is hitting the notes, then we are just making noise. We do this together in community so we are all on the same page, just like when a team comes together right before hitting the football field or basketball court. Singing is supposed to be a horizontal activity with a vertical focus.

The mistake most groups make is fostering an atmosphere in their song service that enables people to mentally wander during the song service. It should be irrelevant what it sounds like. It should be very relevant that everyone is encouraged to channel their emotions in the same direction. The song service should be a time for everyone to flush every negative emotion from their minds and focus on God's available power. It should never be about entertainment.

Imagine that someone in our midst is mute and cannot vocalize any words, so therefore, she obviously cannot sing. Is her worship limited? No, unless of course you think God hears what we say. Does God have ears or eardrums? God is intertwined with the spirit and soul of believers, so words are irrelevant. I have no doubt that all of us have daydreamed through songs while hitting every note perfectly. We have to remember that the only connection God has with us during these events are the thoughts that run through our minds. Opportunity and need dictate how that flows in and out of our physical and spiritual bank accounts.

Giving

Moses taught the children of Israel that they should tithe; that is, they should give 10 percent of their goods beginning with the first fruits. This was an appropriate teaching for them; however, for us that teaching is 90 percent short. As we discussed before, they were to give 10 percent whether they wanted to or not. Our instructions are about what goes through our minds related to giving. People could give 90 percent of everything they have but then use the other 10 percent to do anything they wanted to. That would be wrong on any number of levels. The mistake people make is thinking that giving is only related to what is put in the collection plates of the local church. Of course, the local church isn't going to correct that thinking because it would be counterproductive to its own end.

If money tithing is taught in the church, shouldn't time tithing be taught as well? If we are going to follow those instructions about giving, shouldn't we also spend the same the amount of time studying Scripture? If that were the case, we would spend at least16.8 hours each week in Bible study or a total of 873 hours per year, meaning that we could study through the entire Bible every month. What would that be worth? By definition, if people aren't doing that, it is because they don't see the value in doing it. If people thought reading the Bible would lead them to a buried treasure, they would stay up nights and weekends pouring over it. Let's mentally run with that. If time were currency, how much time should we spend in Bible study? Watching television? Being on the computer? What would a pie chart of our time look like? Jesus said it best: "Where your treasure is ..." (Matt. 6:21 NIV).

This illustrates that the way we interpret the whole giving thing is way off base. For example, how much do you love your husband or wife? Here, let's put a percentage on it: 10 percent, 50 percent, or 90 percent? Any of these answers will put you in the doghouse or give you a night on the couch. How much access to that person's spirit will any of those percentages get you? The same is true for accessing God's power. Giving money, time, emotions, or love has never been about tithing. It is about either being all in or not, with no middle ground to claim. We also wouldn't tithe our time with our children. Why then would we even think about just tithing our money toward becoming like God? Giving is never about what we put in the collection plate. Giving is about using the spiritual capital in our minds to decide how best to use the financial capital in our wallets.

The Lord's Supper
Even though the Lord's Supper was intended to create the most vivid imagery for believers, it has become the mother of all rituals in the church. There are so many rules and regulations about the meal that Jesus instituted for His followers in that upper room that it is almost nothing like the way it was intended to be. Jesus

gave thanks for it; therefore, it is a thanksgiving meal. However, gratitude is not something that can actually be scheduled, so the opportunity to share gratitude for the things done for us should begin the moment we arrive. The meal should just be a focused time to share with each other the objects of that gratitude.

The Jews in that upper room were remembering with gratitude the Passover, which commemorated their freedom from Egypt. After observing the Passover, Jesus took what was already there on the table and instituted a slightly different observance than the Passover but with Him playing the role of the Passover lamb. That would make more sense just a few hours later.

There are two realities for the Passover lamb. First, it must be perfect and without defect. Second, its blood through its death would represent salvation for the people. Jesus did not go around during His ministry noting that so far He had lived a perfect life. However, now at the end of His life, He equated Himself to the Passover lamb. The bread represented His perfection, which qualified Him to be the Passover lamb, while the fruit of the vine represented the blood of that sacrificial lamb that was put over the doorpost in Egypt that Jesus was about to replicate on the cross. Imagine that a memorial service is scheduled for a fallen soldier who gave his life for his unit. Whatever else is associated with that time together, there will be emotions flowing both for the loss of life as well as for the lives that were saved. This is how the Lord's Supper should be observed—not as a ritual of things we have to do but as things we get to do to help us focus on the job at hand as we go out into the world to glorify God.

The Lord's Supper is not about unleavened bread and wine or grape juice, although they are appropriate mnemonics. It is about using those memory devices to remember how we have all pledged our lives in memory of the Son of God who saved us and who we are trying to be more like. It is bewildering to me how the Lord's Supper became this somber time of reflection by ourselves. It is about Jesus' death, but it isn't like He is still dead. He is alive! Let's act like it. It should be a time of celebration, not some quiet time where we try to exclude everyone else from our periphery. If we want to have a somber time remembering Jesus' death, we can do that at home. When we come together, it should be about the team coming together and remembering things we never saw or experienced. It should be a joyful occasion that encourages everyone there to be more focused in the coming week and to be more like the One who died for us.

Rituals grow faith in children because it shrinks God enough for them to get their arms around Him, but these same rituals kill faith in older children and young adults for the same reason. When reasons become rituals, those reasons eventually become irrelevant. At the church's inception, there were reasons for doing everything related to the church as the apostles' challenge was to grow faith in barren fields. For anything we currently do in the church that people can daydream through, those items either need to be ended or the people informed so they understand the reasons for doing so. Otherwise, this generation of young people will find their own reasons for doing what they think is most important. It is hard enough to believe in things other rational people do not without adding a religious firewall to the process. There should not be a single ritual used in the church without an extremely relevant reason to do it. Whenever reasons become rituals, then those reasons are no longer valid.

As you continue your discussion about faith with the college student walking with us, how will you explain what our time together should look like? What is the purpose of coming together in the first place and are we accomplishing that goal?

If our time together does not inspire us and encourage us in the most passionate way possible to pursue God's nature with every fiber of our being, then does it matter which kinds of songs are sung or whether an instrument is played? Does it matter whether people are entertained or the place is rocking or not if people aren't ultimately inspired to lift each other up? When that doesn't happen, then that worship service is a waste of time. On the other hand, whatever fuel is needed to emotionally connect everyone in the audience together to facilitate spiritual growth should be available at every service. For our lives, that would maximize what God is worth.

CHAPTER 14

Misunderstanding the Holy Spirit

The topic of the Holy Spirit always seems to be controversial in nature within the church. As previously noted, God is the most misunderstood character in the Bible, but it certainly stands to reason that the Holy Spirit would be second in line for that distinction. Perhaps it's the fact that the King James translation called it the Holy Ghost, which gave it its mysterious aspect hundreds of years ago, putting it in the realm of all the other scary and mysterious things. The fact that Jesus' disciples were still misguided, anticipating a military revolution from their leader only ten days before the Holy Spirit appeared on Pentecost, tells us a lot about why the Holy Spirit came in the first place. If even Jesus couldn't explain Jehovah God to these fishermen, He sure couldn't explain everything that was about to happen to launch this global introduction of God to these same disciples.

When Moses went up Mt. Sinai to receive the Ten Commandments, he could have simply taken a pen and some papyrus and written down what God dictated. Of course, had he done that, the people would have speculated that the words he wrote were his own and not God's, leaving people to their own interpretation. To authenticate the origin of these commands, God carved the words Himself in stone so there would be no question as to their origin and therefore, their intent. This is also why these stone tablets as well as a jar of manna and Aaron's rod that budded were placed in the Ark of the Covenant. They were articles of authentication. It probably would have been better if they could have just had a video of God parting the Red Sea or all the plagues in Egypt, but technology being what it was meant that those three items would have to do for show and tell. The purpose of the Holy Spirit was for exactly the same reason.

The Holy Spirit was sent on the day of Pentecost to prove the words and actions of a few fishermen, a tax collector, and some of their friends could have only come from God. As the power of God spread throughout the world via its believers, there would be more stories to tell and more evidence to authenticate that all of this was solely from God, with the Ark of the Covenant being the template. The Holy Spirit, through miraculous deeds, provided verification that the oral law about Jesus that His followers were spreading was true until the oral law could become written law by the pens of those empowered by the Authenticator.

In the sixteenth chapter of Luke, when the rich man asked Abraham to send Lazarus back from the dead so his brothers would believe, Abraham told him that the written authentication from Moses and the prophets was sufficient for faith. Once the authentication of the codicil to God's Will was committed to writing late in the first century, then the need for authentication through miraculous events became unnecessary. At that point, they would not only have Moses and the prophets as their source of faith, but they would also have the words of Matthew, Mark, Luke, John, etc., to provide eyewitness accounts of God's handiwork. The Holy Spirit came to confirm for Jews that the codicil to God's will was authentic. The Holy Spirit came to confirm for Gentiles that Jehovah God was the supreme God.

Of course, the Holy Spirit is just another way of describing God. The apostle Paul acknowledged in his second letter to the Corinthians that God is the Spirit (2 Cor. 3:17).The Holy Spirit is not separate from God; the Holy Spirit is God. Throughout the Old Testament, God's Spirit is referred to as the Spirit of God, the Spirit of the Lord, the Holy Spirit, His Holy Spirit, the Spirit of the sovereign Lord, and the Spirit. The problem is that God does not have a spirit; God is Spirit. It would be redundant to say that there is a spirit of a spirit. It may have taken fifty years after Jesus ministry for John to have recalled the words of Jesus as He answered the question of the woman at the well about where they should worship God: Mt. Gerazim or Jerusalem. That question might have seemed stupid to John before the Romans turned Jerusalem into a parking lot in AD 70 during the first Jewish revolt, but when worship in Jerusalem became impossible after the destruction of Jerusalem, John related what should have already been obvious: God is Spirit. Of course, he could have never written this while Jerusalem was still the center of his boyhood religion. That is probably why Matthew, Mark, and Luke did not include the story of the woman at the well in their narratives.

By definition, the children of Israel were clueless about God as they were about to enter the Promised Land, so Moses painted a picture of two aspects of God for these children of Israel that started in his first two sentences. One aspect was that God created the heavens and the earth. It was God who carved out the Ten Commandments into stone and who came down to Mt. Sinai and commanded that anyone who touched the mountain would surely die. The other aspect of God Moses presented to the children of Israel was that it was the Spirit of God that hovered upon the face of the deep. Notice that Moses painted God in the vein of other gods the people would have been familiar with from their parents' days in Egypt: untouchable by humans, high and mighty. Notice also that he painted the Spirit of God as intertwining into the hearts and minds of His people. The children of Israel were neophytes concerning their knowledge of God, so Moses had to give these children something about God to wrap their arms around since He wouldn't be available to continue teaching them once they arrived in the Promised Land.

On the day of Pentecost, when it was time to launch this approximately seventy-year period of authentication about the update to God's will and testament, it was simply God's power that launched this activity, not some separate Holy Spirit. The inordinate power of the creating force of the universe would intimately work within the minds of Jesus' disciples to begin the transformation away from a culture of superstition around the world to a love-based, compassion-based way of life intended to permeate the world. The Holy Spirit was an effective teaching mnemonic to help these simple fishermen and a tax collector understand the miraculous things that were about to happen.

The apostles were not theologians or scholars; in fact, they were clueless about Jesus' mission even as Jesus was ascending into heaven. God created the heavens and the universe; God parted the Red Sea; God wrote the Ten Commandments in stone; and God equipped His disciples with power on Pentecost to authenticate the things Jesus had set in motion. To simplify the sales pitch that these fishermen were to use in spreading the good news, God was personified as the Holy Spirit (Comforter, Counselor) to verify that what they were selling was true. By compartmentalizing God like Moses did for the Israelites, it became easier for everyone to grasp the source of the power.

There are churches today that teach the Holy Spirit comes when one is baptized although they cannot explain how that happens or the biological connection between being dipped in water and God's Spirit entering a person. Neither can they explain to a child or teenager who had believed in God their whole life why they did not feel anything special upon their baptism. Salvation is solely related to faith as a biological reality where the mind accepts God and then harnesses His power through faith in that Spirit. Baptism is a physical act intended to define a spiritual threshold of faith. Baptism is not done so an omniscient God will become aware of a person's faith and commitment. Simply put, baptism symbolizes to the participant and to others that a permanent threshold has been crossed. That is because once it is accomplished, it cannot be undone. After all, a person can be unbaptized but he or she cannot *become* unbaptized any more than a person can *become* uncircumcised. Abraham was circumcised as a seal of faith, a threshold to cross indicating a permanent bond. Circumcism, for Christians, was replaced with baptism to make it universal for all believers for obvious reasons. The paradox is that although baptism has nothing to do with salvation, a person cannot be saved without it because of the threshold of faith it defines. Where there is no faith, there can be no salvation. That is why for every generation since the apostles lived, faith in God (rather than baptism) activates the Spirit of God within us to do incredible things.

During the launch period of Christianity, the Holy Spirit was imparted solely by God and the apostles to authenticate God's power through miraculous gifts, whether or not their faith was ready for it (1 Cor. 12-14). Before the apostles laid their hands on the people, those people had no miraculous gifts, yet afterward they did. As Paul noted, in a perfect world, a gardener would work diligently to grow fruit. Through faith in God and in what He is doing and careful attention, the fruit grows accordingly.

That was not what happened during the power of authentication. People instantly had fruit (gifts) without knowing how to garden, evidenced especially by the church in Corinth. Once people empowered by God's Spirit could provide an orderly written account and testimonial about this addendum to God's will, the authentication provided by God's Spirit would become unnecessary as the perfect replaced the imperfect. At that point, God's Spirit could grow in His people unchecked and unbounded, commensurate with their faith rather than by a miraculous gift. Luke noted to Theophilus that people received the gift of the Holy Spirit when the apostles, themselves, laid their hands on believers (Acts 8:17-19; Acts 19:6). Even Paul noted to believers that had been baptized in Rome that he longed to come to them and impart spiritual gifts to make them strong (Romans 1:11).

Luke is careful in the words he chose to note that people who were not apostles such as Philip, Aquila, Priscilla and Apollos, no matter how strong the gift of the Holy Spirit moved in them, that they could not impart the gift of the Spirit to anyone. For example, when Luke provided some background information about the Greek "deacons" (all seven had Greek names) selected to help the Greek widows being neglected in Jerusalem, he noted two specially gifted men, Stephen and Philip, who were full of the Holy Spirit. After Stephen's death, Philip, who could perform miraculous deeds, went to Samaria to preach and baptized several people into the name of Jesus but none of them received the gift of the Holy Spirit upon their baptism. This man was Philip the Evangelist, a great man full of the Holy Spirit with great power who raised four daughters who became prophetesses. Luke would have known all about Philip and his family because Paul's entourage spent many nights in Philip's house (Acts 21:8) so the things that Luke wrote about would have been straight from the horse's mouth. If there was ever a non-apostle who could have imparted the gift of the Spirit it would have been Philip. However, nowhere in scripture does it state that Philip ever imparted the Holy Spirit to anyone.

Whenever the Holy Spirit was received, an apostle was in the middle of the receipt. Today, we all possess God's Spirit to the degree our faith enables. For someone to believe that we "receive" the gift of the Holy Spirit today, that person has to also believe that Philip was able to impart the Holy Spirit in the first century.

You may have noticed that today there are no apostles, and therefore, there are no miraculous gifts. However, I do know several people whose spirit is empowered by God living in them to do incredible and even supernatural things. We are people of God, so we are by definition people of supernatural things and events. The things that are possible when God lives in us are unlimited and even far greater than anything that ever happened during the authentication period. Moving mountains would not even be a challenge for us when God lives in us.

What do you believe about the Holy Spirit as it relates biologically to God's followers? What can you explain about it to young people trying to understand it? Where was it on the day before Pentecost? Would Ananias and Sapphira have died if they did what they did today? How does the Holy Spirit metaphysically differ from God? Jesus is alive, but is He alive physically or spiritually or both? How would you explain that?

The Holy Spirit is still a good teaching device for Jesus' followers today. It is appropriate to teach children about the Holy Spirit to help them better understand God, just as Santa Claus is used to teach children about the spirit of Christmas. If it was appropriate for the neophytes of the first century to use something to help them better understand God at their level of understanding, then it's appropriate for the neophytes of the twenty-first century to use the same device. However, as adults it may be more beneficial to focus on growing in the knowledge of God so God's power can grow exponentially in us, with turning the world upside down being the goal. Faith in God is the portal through which God overwhelms our spirits to do supernatural things, and God is a whole lot bigger and more powerful than Scripture could ever capture. That is why training aids were used. As faith grows, God's power grows in direct proportion as the flesh gives way to Spirit. As teenagers and young adults experience that power, they will be drawn to its source.

Whether it pertains to God or athletics, people's spirits are filled with whatever they are pursuing. It is not related to what they are supposed to be pursuing or what they wish they were pursuing; it is solely related to whatever their minds are consumed with. This is the biochemistry and metaphysics of the spirit that reside within us and what we attach to it. When God lives in us, what actually happens within our physical being? When our favorite sports team lives in us, what actually happens within our physical being? It is a misnomer to say that anyone is filled with God's Spirit because as long as we are wearing this suit of humanity, there will always be a hole in our bucket, constantly draining it out. Actually, God doesn't fill anyone with His Spirit anyway. God makes His Spirit available to anyone who is willing to take ownership of it and then lets their faith pump in whatever of God their faith can hold, like a filling station.

CHAPTER 15 —

This Sandbox Called Life

No matter what a person's age, everyone seems to enjoy playing in the sand. Whether it is simply taking a walk on the beach or making giant sand castles or anything in between, there just seems to be something cathartic about experiencing sand.

None of us probably remember the first time our parents let us play in the sand, but it may have been at some nearby playground that happened to have a sandbox for children to play together in. There may have been toy cars and trucks to roll through the sand, or there may have been toy rakes and shovels to create your own little world. Most children know how to share and play nice, but there are always some kids who pick on other kids just because they don't know how not to. They may even take toys away from other kids. Although we may not understand it at the time, life in the sandbox can eerily mimic the rest of our lives as well.

Many times in our lives we have heard that life isn't fair or that life is what you make of it. That doesn't really help children process the bullies they may encounter or the things in their lives that may fall apart. After all, it isn't their fault when their parents' marriages fail or loved ones die. Life may be what you make of it, but for many people, it still can be more than they can bear. The thing that tends to get missed when considering why good or bad things happen to people is that many times the forks in the road that brought us to where we currently are were based on good and bad decisions that may have happened several generations previously. Decisions about whom to marry, where to live, and even which road to take to a given event can change the course of lives for generations to come. The most important aspect of Christianity relates to life's decision-making process for those who believe.

The author of the book of Job gives us our first look in the Bible at the evil character named Satan. Satan was later named Beelzebub, whom we first met in the Old Testament as a Philistine god (2 Kings 1:2). I guess it should not be surprising that a Philistine god in the Old Testament became a Jewish devil in the New Testament. Moses never named the serpent in his garden story, so over time and because of the prophecy, the serpent became associated with this name as well. The apostle Peter metaphorically noted to his audience that Satan prowls around like a roaring lion seeking to devour, although he never defined how exactly Satan does that.

Just as God is personified in Scripture, Satan is also personified by noting that he walked to and fro over the earth. I hope he had a good pair of shoes. By definition of this personification, the author was helping his audience grasp concepts that were absent in previous writings.

The book of Job describes two conversations Satan had with God about the goodness of a man named Job concerning the origin and source of that goodness. Job was a righteous man who followed God's will as he led his family in serving God. The first conversation between God and Satan included God highlighting Job's faithfulness. Because God's covenant to the children of Israel said bad things wouldn't happen if they were good, then by definition, Job's righteousness was keeping Satan at bay. During this discussion, God seemingly waived the covenant, and as long as Job wasn't touched, Satan could unload all of the torture he could muster. Imagine that when God told Satan he could do anything to Job but not touch him or kill him, Satan went ahead and killed him anyway. I guess that would have ended the story. But we know that in the story of Job, Satan was given boundaries to help relate the story the author intended.

Job and his wife had seven sons and three daughters who would have meant the world to them. One by one, each of them was needlessly killed, meaning that Job and his wife would have felt more pain than any human should ever have to feel. This didn't just happen to Job; Job's wife also had to endure the loss of her cherished family. There were no pictures to remember them by and no explanations. We know at the end of this story, they had ten more children, but the original children are gone, and they were never coming back. Their pain for these children lasted forever. We know the second part of this story involves Job having boils. Compared with the loss of his ten children, the boils were nothing.

As Job's wife watched him suffer from the loss of all their property, all of their children, and having his body inflicted with boils from his head to his toes, she couldn't help but hope for the end to his suffering. There is no doubt she was suffering too, but her pain wasn't included in this discussion. She begged him to curse God and die even though it would have left her all alone. Then three of Job's friends came to visit him and almost gagged at his appearance and suffering and sat with him for a week before their curiosity got the better of them. Since the covenant with God stated that if you do good, good things will happen, and if you do bad, bad things will happen, they were quite certain this would qualify as something very, very bad, so they begged Job to tell them what bad thing he had done. This interpretation of the covenant persisted even until Jesus' time so that when His followers saw a blind man, they wondered who sinned, his parents or himself.

Job's friends relentlessly asked him to confess his sin so God might have mercy on him. After listening to his wife beg him to curse God and die, as well as having these friends lecture him about confessing something he hadn't done, Job couldn't take it anymore. After being worn down by his wife and his friends, Job exclaimed to his friends (paraphrasing Job 31:6): "I haven't done anything to deserve this!" Seemingly adding to Job's pain, God scolded Job about trying to justify himself.

What kind of God is this? What kind of God do we serve? Every time there is a tragedy, those are the types of questions many people ask. By definition, when we constantly ask these types of questions any time a terrorist strikes or devastation occurs, it means we still really don't have a clue about God or about how the sandbox of life was constructed.

The Boundaries of Evil
First of all, in real life, evil has no such boundaries. Just like the mind has the ability to grow and develop attributes that can promote God's power on the earth for generations, the mind can

also become victim to addiction and abuse, leading to the lowest form of evil. This can cause depravity of unlimited proportions, which feeds on itself and can leave death and destruction in its wake. Of course, the purpose of the story of Job was not to define the boundaries of good and evil but rather to further define God's relationship with His people. Moses wrote to the children of Israel the same thing we tell our children when they are young: if you do good, good things will happen, and if you do bad, bad things will happen. In the story of Job, we see the natural maturing and evolution of our understanding of God: if you do good, bad things may happen, but good things can still evolve from the bad things.

The other lesson to learn from Job's story is that good has no boundaries, either. As we have discussed, the mind is limitless, and therefore, God's Spirit living in us is also limitless. We just have to unlearn the boundaries. Growing in spirit and thereby in spiritual strength allows us to compete against evil and be victorious. You will note that the book of Job is written in a poetic format. Since Satan was saddled with restrictions that evil itself does not have, it simply provides us with a glimpse of the battle between good and evil but not necessarily the battle itself. Realizing that evil has no defined boundaries should make our pursuit of spiritual strength all the more intense.

The story of Job was written to give hope and encouragement to godly people who were suffering in their pursuit of God. It was intended to let them know that their misery wasn't caused by their ungodliness. To the children of Israel entering the Promised Land, this elementary teaching became their mantra to keep them on the straight and narrow. The bond between righteousness and blessings was the focus of the Law. As the

Israelites grew in the knowledge of God, that interpretation needed to be updated as their understanding of God would have grown with it. The story of Job provided that instruction in a very powerful way.

This brings us to another fork in the road as we need to decide whether the stories in the Bible about Satan are literal or whether they are figurative or metaphoric. If they are literal, then we need to be able to explain how Satan tries to tempt seven billion people at the same time and how Satan biologically prowls around like a roaring lion. If they are figurative accounts of the power of evil on earth, then what are the actual boundaries of evil God's people face every day? Is it Satan that tempts people in their addictions or is it dopamine and serotonin or other biological realities that lead us in the wrong direction? Is Satan a metaphor for evil so young children can better understand temptation? In biblical times, would people with dementia and epilepsy have been considered to have demons or be possessed with demons? Is temptation to sin a mental reality or coercion from an evil being?

The authors of Scripture handled this in different ways depending on their audience. For example, Peter did note to his Jewish audience scattered throughout Pontus, Galatia, Cappadocia, Asia and Bithynia that Satan does prowl around like a roaring lion while Paul wrote similar words to some of the churches he instructed. However, when Paul wrote to the church in Rome, the center of the universe and a church he was obviously trying to impress, evidenced by the big words he used in this letter, he discarded the Satan metaphor for evil he had used in letters to other churches and just used evil to describe the antithesis of God. It is interesting to note that Paul never referred to Satan anywhere in his letter to Rome except in his farewell comments.

No matter how these questions are answered, the bottom line is that God resides in the mind, and therefore the fight between good and evil actually takes place inside oneself and not up in the sky. As such, sin is a mental and biological phenomenon rather than an event. Being able to withstand temptation from any front requires a strong mind to guard the treasure. Therefore, that is the goal in any spiritual exercise program: having a strong mind.

Where Is God?

Halfway between Louisville and Cincinnati on Interstate 71 at mile marker 40, there is a sign that commemorates a tragic accident that occurred several years ago. The sign that remembers that event reads: "Site of Fatal Bus Accident on May 14, 1988." On that date, a bus full of children and teenagers from a church group was returning from a day of fun at Kings Island theme park when a drunk driver hit them head-on at that location after having gotten on the interstate going the wrong direction. Twenty-seven people were killed, dozens were injured, and others were scarred for life from the flames. The drunk driver, whose blood alcohol level was three times today's legal limit, survived. Even though it has now been twenty-four years since the accident, the emotional scars for the parents who lost their children on that day will never go away.

Just like in the story of Job, we want to ask God why He let this happen. If the bus had just been a couple of seconds earlier or later, then maybe those children would not have perished. Why didn't it happen to the car ahead or behind this bus, sparing the lives of children who faithfully believed in God? Those children never got to grow up or have families of their own. The pain their parents felt would last them a lifetime, affecting many of their decisions to come. Those who were tragically injured have to bear the scars of something that wasn't their fault, and by definition, the accident altered the lives of hundreds of people for several generations. The course of life was altered for every person involved in this senseless accident. What kind of God would let this happen? Is He not powerful enough to have prevented it? Why were believers killed instead of nonbelievers?

Perhaps not to the same degree, all of us at some point in our lives, if not at multiple points, will be called upon to cross bridges for which we are unprepared—tumors and tornados, accidents and evil, death and destruction. This is exactly the opposite of the things that Moses promised would happen to the Israelites as they entered the Promised Land. Doing good does not guarantee bad things in this life won't happen. Why do these bad things happen today as we are trying to follow God? To begin to understand why bad things happen to good people and why it seems that sometimes God intervenes and sometimes He doesn't, we have to bear in mind the nature of God.

At the beginning of the book of Job, Job was very religious, to a fault. He made sacrifices for his kids just in case they forgot. He had an idea of who God was, but actually he was clueless about God. Job was going on the picture Moses had painted for the Israelites.

At the end of this poem, after God gives us a dissertation about why the covenant no longer involves "if you do good ..." and as we learn more about God than Moses could possibly have related to the wandering Israelites, Job gives us a haunting realization. Job says that at the beginning of this ordeal he thought he knew God, but at the end, he noted that now he knew God (Job 42:5). Before, God was a religious and almost superstitious symbol. At the end, Job knew the power of the one true and living God. Job's possessions were doubled from what he had previously owned, but God only gave him the same number of children. Why would God double Job's possessions but not his children? The previous possessions were all lost, but his children were not; God had them.

So what is the lesson to be learned from all Scripture has to teach us about God? Why do bad things happen to good people? The answer is simple, although none of us want to hear it: God only cares about our development as spiritual beings in a physical world. As such, we are free to set our own training schedule and environment so we control the pace of the lessons and the majority of their outcome. God made this world and everything in it as our sandbox from which to learn about God. In the sandbox, we learn to share and care. However, toys can get broken in the sandbox.

The sole mission of our existence is to glorify God, and how we take the things in this sandbox to learn about God or not is up to us. How we live is up to us. God put in this sandbox oxygen, aluminum, sand, gold, gravel, uranium, and all of the other elements and things for us to educate ourselves as we learn more about God. He set in motion worlds that are light years away to give mankind more toys to play with for millions of years to come as more of these worlds are discovered. Like it or not, the decisions and life choices our ancestors made have affected our lives, and the choices we make will affect generations to come. To put this in some perspective, God said He would take care of all of our needs but said nothing about our wants. It is how we deal with our wants that determine much of the course of our lives.

Toys in the Sandbox

If you have a young child, you will use an assortment of things to teach your child, but you don't care about the things; you only care about training your child. When we build nuclear power plants, there may be consequences in our training. When we build cars and roads and bridges, there may be consequences. There is an outcome for everything we try—sometimes good, sometimes bad. God has made Himself available to cram as much of Him as possible into ourselves to help us in this journey, and when we don't do that, there are consequences. When the generations before us didn't do that, there were consequences for everyone down the line. Even though the children killed in the bus crash couldn't do anything about it, perhaps had the people in the life of the driver filled themselves full of God, he might have had a different outcome by making different life choices. There is enough of God to go around and fill the world with His nature thousands of times over.

When we transfer ownership of our minds to God, we can move mountains and change the world. As we learned from Josiah's lesson, we won't be able to grab a bare electrical wire and keep from electrocuting ourselves or break any other law of biology or physics without repercussions, but God living in us changes the way we live. We'll take those odds. And when we do draw the short end of the stick, God is there in our minds as our faith allows to comfort us and remind us of where Job's kids are.

God set up the sandbox of life a long time ago. He may not care about the sand, but He certainly cares an awful lot about us in that He sent His Son who grew up in the sandbox to show us how to play in it in a way nobody had ever demonstrated before. Some bullies killed Him for doing this, which makes us grateful for the life He lived and the life He gave. The purpose of Scripture is to show us how to get the most out of the sandbox and alter the course of history so those who will play in it long after we are through will be able to marvel at the way its Maker constructed it.

CHAPTER 16

When the Music Stops

In any classroom in America, there will be some children in the class motivated by the anticipation of a reward, while others can be best influenced by the threat of punishment. Determining what motivates each student takes some investment on the part of the teacher. It probably isn't very hard for any of us, no matter how old we are, to remember back to our elementary school years. For all of us, there would have certainly been times when our teacher might have been called to the principal's office to handle some administrative duty, which meant that for some period of time, we would have been left alone while she was gone. If the absence would have only been for a few seconds, then she might not have thought much about giving us behavioral instruction while she was gone. But imagine when we were in second grade that our teacher had to be gone, say, for five minutes? Fifteen minutes? Thirty minutes? What if our second-grade teacher had to be gone for an hour with no other supervision available to look in on us? Imagine the extreme threats of punishment the teacher would have given us to encourage our best behavior while she was gone.

She would have also promised great rewards to us if she found us doing as we were told when she returned. Of course, we would not know exactly when she was coming back. There is no doubt that one of the things she would have told us before she left, no matter how long she was going to be gone, is that we needed to behave because she was coming right back—that she was coming back soon. This scenario describes the book of Revelation in its entirety.

For centuries Bible scholars and theologians have been trying to unravel the mysteries presented in John's Revelation but by definition, have failed in this endeavor because they haven't read the book in its context. Let's start by imagining at the beginning of time that God had set the time of Jesus' return to be that of August 12 in the year of AD 854,367. If that were the case, should a single word of Scripture need to be changed? No, not when read in its context. At a time when the Thessalonians were despairing about the numerous deaths among them, would Paul have tried to encourage them by exclaiming about the immediacy of the rapture as he did if he knew that Jesus wasn't going to return for at least two thousand years? Probably not, because his sole intention for writing this letter was to light a fire under them to remain strong in the face of extreme adversity and to reassure them in their choice of Christianity. Paul was not giving them a dissertation on theology; he was providing them an anchor to hold onto when times got tough. You may have noticed that what he told the Thessalonians about the Rapture never happened nor have the events John described in his Revelation happened either.

When Jesus ascended into heaven, His disciples kept looking at the sky, perhaps thinking He was coming right back down.

The men in white standing there with them had to break the news to them that there was a different plan. When considering the writings of Luke, Paul, and John, probably every generation since Jesus left has thought Jesus was coming back during their lifetime. This is still the case today. The Teacher is certainly coming back soon, as He said, but just as the second-grade class missed the teacher's point, so has every generation since Jesus' ascension missed the point of John's writings.

John's Revelation is, without a doubt, the most ingenious letter ever written. No matter how many times I read it, I am always amazed at its wisdom, its power, its universality, and its encouragement to any generation trying to live a godly life. It is a message of faith, hope, and love conveyed by the man Jesus loved. Therefore, he would fully understand the depths of love and how to convey it in his old age. How could anything John wrote be anything else? But it is not a book about foretelling the future even though John himself tells his audience or more appropriately, his exilers, that it is a book of prophecy. The context shows that it is simply a letter of love and encouragement set against the canvas of the world's conflicts intended to highlight the way home.

For those of us who were alive when President John F. Kennedy was assassinated, those events penetrated the emotions and memories of anyone old enough to remember. Even though it has now been fifty years since its occurrence, anyone who watched the news accounts and videos of the aftermath probably has them frozen in time in their minds. I can remember being in the fourth grade waiting for the end of the school day. It was the Wednesday before Thanksgiving so we were about to be out of school for four days. About 1:00 PM the principal of our school walked into our classroom and told everyone that the president had been shot. We spent the rest of the school day watching television as news accounts told the sad news that our president had been killed. That day, the television was used to burn memories into the minds of children not able to understand how the world in the 1960's was about to change.

Although those emotions are still fresh for anyone affected, it is impossible to transmit those emotions to subsequent generations so that they can feel the power of that loss. Time has a way of dampening the emotional connection of sanguine events so that eventually the only things left are the lessons to be learned from those events. I'm sure the same thing happened for the generation of Americans who experienced Abraham Lincoln's death or Pearl Harbor's attack and will likely happen for generations to come about major events of the past few years.

When John penned his letter of encouragement to churches in Asia Minor, it had been about the same fifty year time lapse since Jesus ascended in the sky as it has been for us since President Kennedy was killed, meaning that some of the emotional connection would have, by definition, diminished. There were no videos of Jesus' crucifixion, nor a set of tapes capturing his teachings so those mental images would need to be continually redrawn, especially for the Gentile audience that dominated his field of vision in Asia Minor. John was inspired to recharge the batteries of his troops but he had some major obstacles to overcome.

To put it in proper context, we have to first transport John to the island of Patmos, a place he would rather not have been. John noted that he was there because of the Word of God.

Another man named John who baptized people also spent time in jail because of the Word of God, and he was killed because of it. Jesus was killed because of the gospel. Paul was shipwrecked, beaten, and stoned because of the gospel. It is no wonder that John was exiled to Patmos because of the gospel. A passion for God's Word will have that effect on a hostile world. Whether it was the Romans or the Ephesians who put him there, the fact that he was exiled there says many things.

First of all, they could have just killed him, but John probably had rock star status among the faithful, so making him a martyr would have likely only fanned the flames they were trying to extinguish. We saw from Luke's account that the Ephesians were very fussy about anyone upsetting their economic apple cart, so it would not be surprising for John in his old age to be driving them crazy in his pursuit of trying to live like his friend Jesus. After all, do we know any old people today who don't say what is on their minds? Instead of killing the infection, John's captors just removed it, so off to nearby Patmos John was taken.

Life in Exile

Being in exile didn't mean that John was sitting on the beach waiting for the next snorkeling expedition. His captors put him there for a reason, and the people who put him there sure would not have allowed him to stir up trouble while in exile. Any correspondence he might have sent would have certainly been censored. In writing about his revelation, he had to have known the first people to read it would have been his captors.

For each of the seven churches, John wrote words from Jesus in the first three chapters that concentrate on those churches doing a better job of the religion they profess. Neither the Ephesians nor the Roman Empire would have had a problem with religion as long as that religion didn't impact the commerce of Ephesus, so his instructions to those churches would not have been offensive—entertaining but not offensive.

It is interesting to note that Jesus only addressed the churches in Asia Minor. He didn't mention the churches at Rome, Philippi, Thessalonica, or Corinth, and surely these churches had things they needed to work on too. The reason John wrote about the churches in Asia and not the other churches is that when John had to leave Jerusalem when the Romans turned it under, he apparently settled in Asia Minor. These were the people he needed to encourage because if it was tough when the tree was green (Jesus' metaphor), imagine how difficult it would have been to stay true to Christ's teachings once John was taken away. This region needed a shoulder to cry on as well as a kick in the pants to encourage them to hold on until the end, but John was not there to help them. What could John possibly do to light a fire under his fellow soldiers that could get past the censors to inspire them to diligently follow God's will? How would you have done it?

First of all, the Gentiles in Ephesus would not likely have been familiar with an abandoned fort in Israel called Tel Meggido. During our visit to Israel, we got to walk all over this hill and through its cistern and then stand at the top of it, looking out over the fertile land below. This tel (hill) would have provided ample warning against invading armies while providing cover against attack. At the time John wrote his letter from Patmos, Meggido had been a deserted fortress and outpost for several hundred years. It would have been very familiar to

Israelites since it sits along the route leading from the sea to all places east. Later excavations uncovered 24 distinct layers of civilization from its history so Meggido, at some previous point in time, played an important role in the people of this region. Like a great film maker, John chose to use it as the backdrop of a great battle he would tell the churches in Asia Minor. This metaphoric war between good and evil would take place at Tel Megiddo: Armageddon.

In the first three chapters of his letter, John encouraged each congregation by name as to what they needed to do to better follow the religion they had chosen. John then wrote an incredible Halloween story that the censors would have been amused at but the faithful would have been encouraged by. For eighteen chapters, John poked a stick in the eye of Rome, for which the faithful would have cheered, but the Romans would not have understood it. It is important to remember that during the time when John would have written this letter, the emperors of Rome were implementing emperor worship, making Christianity more difficult and costly to practice. The stakes were already extremely high in the choices Christians were forced to make.

As previously noted, the sole reason John's Revelation was written was to encourage the troops back home in Asia Minor. Whether it was Peter warming himself by the fire two thousand years ago or adversity striking today, the evaporation rate of faith is directly related to its cost. The cost at the time John wrote this was high. He pulled out all stops in this letter to get it by the censors and effectively rally those who were wavering.

This brings us to our last fork in the road. What do you believe about the end of time and how can you explain it to someone whose faith is wavering? Why didn't the Rapture happen in their lifetime as Paul told the Thessalonians it would? Was Paul wrong? Is it okay to say that an apostle was wrong? Is it necessary for the things written in the Book of Revelation to ever happen? What date will "soon" expire letting us know that this story was metaphoric? As we consider all of the forks in the road presented in this study, it is important that all of the forks and choices made about each topic are able to follow one particular path that makes sense. Like any treasure map, the clues should be interpreted in a way that weaves each of the interpretations into one distinct path toward the treasure. No treasure map allows its followers to pick and choose which interpretation tastes the best in an a la carte fashion. Its path must be seamless as each piece of the puzzle fits the other pieces making the treasure visible.

Why did Jesus use the "soon" language to the troops to try to encourage them to hold on until the end if it wasn't going to happen soon? Well, it is. And it has. When John's intended audience took their last breath, Jesus came. When my grandmother died, Jesus came. When I take my last breath, Jesus will come. As each succeeding generation is born and dies, from now until this world is no more, Jesus came. John wrote about a time when the adversity was so difficult that he asked Jesus to come quickly. John was a master wordsmith in his gospel as well as this letter of encouragement. This letter, which anchors the compilation of the New Testament writings, is certainly a masterpiece. Once we realize it is not a book of prophecy that foretells things but rather a book of prophecy that teaches things, then it is a lot easier to see its wisdom and strength.

God didn't activate star systems that won't even be seen for millions of years just to end this parade after a couple of millennia. Yet people still sell everything they have because they are certain of something that will not occur. Each of us needs to focus on tapping into God's power by feeding our minds spiritual food then God will thrive in our lives. None of us know when soon will come, and our last breath can come at any time. Our goal is to give up on our humanity before it gives up on us. In the end, if we are focused on the goal of faith's intervention in our lives, then it doesn't matter when Jesus comes and we should not be waiting on it. It will come soon enough.

CHAPTER 17

Our Last Day on Earth

It is 4:00 in the morning, and you are awakened by someone standing next to your bed. While you are trying to process this picture, your guest tells you he is an angel sent to inform you that you have exactly twenty-four hours to live and that he will return at precisely 4:00 the next morning to take you home. You announce that this must be some sort of prank being played on you and all of your friends can come out from hiding, having nearly scared you to death. Your guest reiterates that he is an angel sent from God and then proves his identity, leaving no doubt of your fate: you have twenty-four hours to live. The angel then gives some instructions. You can't tell anyone what is about to happen, and you have to go about your normal activities because if you don't follow these instructions, the consequences will be immediate.

There would certainly be a tsunami of emotions that would wash over you. You would experience pure joy knowing you are about to go home to be with God while experiencing the torture of being torn away from the ones you love. Just for today, there will be such an urgency of sharing things that you've kept to yourself as you show love and encouragement to everyone you meet. Just for today, it will be okay if you make a fool of yourself as you touch the lives of the ones you love as you break out of the rut of your everyday life. It is because this day is special; it is because this is your last day on earth. Today, you will be aware of every last detail of life, from the birds chirping and dogs barking to babies crying and children playing. Today, when people say things that would normally upset you, they just roll off your back as you stay focused solely on things that really matter.

Today you will catch yourself crying about things you should have done and fences you should have mended. Today, you will make things right with everyone. Today people will marvel at the joy you possess and will think you've lost your mind. Today you will love others as you have never loved before, and you will lead in the ways you should have always led. Today you will do things according to their importance in your life, with no time for clutter. Today you will hug the ones you love like there is no tomorrow.

After you have spent the entire day focused on it being the only day you have to make an impact in people's lives, you fall asleep, exhausted. At precisely 4:00 a.m., you are awakened by the same guest as he promised. He tells you that you have been given a twenty-four-hour extension and that at precisely four o'clock the next morning, he will return to take you home. Your gratitude for another day is overwhelming. Although you spent the entire day before in a passionate embrace of life, there were still things that could have been done and words that could have been said. So on this day, as the day before, you set out to change the world but perhaps with a little less reckless abandon. It happens this day, then the next day, and then the day after that.

This same scenario continues to play itself out day after day. It is hard to stay as focused as you did on the first day. As the song says, there are planes to catch and bills to pay, so you try to balance the two worlds, but as the urgency wanes, so does the focus. Your visitor keeps coming every morning at four o'clock with the same extension of time. Eventually, you just tune him out and go back to sleep while he speaks his warning since you had a rough evening the night before worrying about how to handle life. After all, it is hard to be at peace when you have to deal with so many problems.

One morning the angel doesn't give you the usual extension of time. On that morning, he tells you it is time to go. You look at him in disbelief, as if you have just seen a ghost. But you can't go yet; you are not ready. The fences you previously mended are broken again. You've been angry and upset at times and need to make things right, but this is to no avail, because it is time to go. Regrets will have to remain regrets, and unspoken words will have to remain unspoken.

Thank goodness this is just an imaginary story. Unfortunately, we won't know when it is our time to go. For those of us who have pledged our lives to the discipline of Christ, we should all be living with the urgency of the last day, leaving nothing undone. Every day we should say whatever needs to be said as if it were our last day on earth. We should not withhold love or encouragement to anyone we encounter every single day. We should touch as many people as possible every day we are given, without regard to whether someone might have hurt our feelings or said something he or she will later regret. Love has no expiration date.

A life dedicated to our Lord should make every day seem

like Christmas, New Year's, and Thanksgiving all rolled into one. Every day we wake up we should act as if the date on the calendar that day is the second one listed on our tombstone. There are no boundaries for people who believe in God and His Son; there are no boundaries for people who focus their full energy in living their eulogy backward.

CHAPTER 18

Learning to Sprint Downhill

At the end of a close football game, the field goal kicker will start getting ready in case he is called on to try to kick the game-winning field goal. Although he will practice a few kicks, there is something else he will be just as focused on as loosening his leg. He will be intently focused on the wind and its direction. Any time a coach contemplates a long field goal, he has to know whether the wind is with him or against him before he sends out his field-goal team for such a long kick. It is a lot easier to kick with the wind behind you than when it is blowing in your face.

A football goes a lot farther with a tailwind. So does a golf ball, a baseball, and even a Frisbee. It is also easier to run downhill than it is to run uphill; that is just physics. For anyone looking for an advantage in life, always look for a tailwind or a downhill sprint. It can be the difference between winning and losing and between success and failure. We all know life is not a sprint but a marathon. But what if you could run the marathon of life at sprinting speed?

The intention of Jesus' teachings for His disciples was to show them how to live their lives running downhill no matter how hard the uphill battle they faced looked on the surface. I guess athletic coaches use the same theology to motivate their teams. Facing adversity is inevitable for everyone, no matter their state of life. How we respond to that adversity is dependent on the foundation that was poured long before the adversity arose. Most coaches will subject their teams to game situations in practice that are much tougher than anything they will ever see during a real game. That way, they will be ready for anything that comes their way. Unfortunately, there are no practice sessions in life. As we all know, life has no mulligans or do-overs, so mistakes made in the game of life leave scars.

Priceless

How much money would it take for you to give up your religion and your faith? That is, how much is your faith worth to you? If someone were to come into your church one Sunday in the middle of the worship service and offer anyone who would agree to not come back for a year one hundred dollars, how many would take it? What if the amount was changed to $1,000? Would that change anyone's mind? Let's take this illustration to the extreme. What if we were offered $1,000,000 to never darken the doors of a church ever again. What is our faith really worth? Why do we really go to church?

If the only reason we go to church has to do with anything other than becoming stronger in the attributes of God, then we are probably wasting our time. That isn't to say there aren't some important interactions between fellow believers that are useful toward that goal, but in the end, if it is just a social encounter, then it isn't accomplishing the goal of being there in the first

place. The sole purpose for being there is to drin
of God's nature as possible with the help of those
the same unbelievable things we believe. There is n
a price on that!

When David confronted Goliath, he already knew he would win unless he was forced to play the game the way others thought it should be played. Had he put on Saul's armor, he would have likely lost. Putting on the armor would have been playing it safe by doing what everyone else thought he should do. However, God doesn't reside in comfort zones. Just as sophisticated equipment must be constantly recalibrated to maximize its effectiveness, prayer for us is a means of continually recalibrating our lives back to the commitment we made to God. Prayer is a time to kick the world into neutral and assess the direction we are headed based on how well we are emulating Christ's example. From cover to cover, the Bible is filled with stories about people who didn't play the odds but followed their logic and their emotions toward an unexpected outcome. People are so starved for leadership that blends wisdom, logic, and emotion toward the common good. That describes leaders like Joshua, Gideon, and Nehemiah, but that list also includes anyone today who is filled with those godly attributes.

If the attributes of God were the pixels that comprised His portrait, then it would take numerous colors of ink to accurately paint His picture. This ink is available to anyone willing to pick up a brush and start painting. Although God has countless attributes, it is appropriate for each of us to zero in on those characteristics most valuable for our lives. There are hundreds of God's attributes available to us; here is a simple list of twenty-five characteristics of God that may be useful to target:

Purity	Generous	Wise
Persistence	Discerning	Gentle
Focus	Truthful	Compassionate
Strength	Patient	Peaceful
Love	Self-Controlled	Forgiving
Endurance	Resolute	Passionate
Sacrifice	Faithful	Fearless
Boundless	Calm	
Consistent	Thorough	

Whether we want to be a great athlete, a good employee, a good servant, or just a good mom or dad, son or daughter, the more of us we allow God to saturate, the more successful at it we will be. We go to church to become like God because the other people in the room likely have incredible strength in some of these qualities they are willing to share. There is one exercise people of faith can do to strengthen God's spirit in them. This exercise becomes more powerful and intimate with a smaller group but it can also be effective in groups of fifty people or more. This exercise begins by selecting any ten attributes of God and then writing each of them on individual sheets of paper, folding them and putting them in a pile. Then have someone pick one of them from the pile and after announcing that attribute, have the group vote to select a person from within that group who possesses that godly trait to the max. The selection process can be by open ballet or silent ballet but once that person is announced, have that person explain what has led them to strength in that godly trait. After sharing what created strength in that attribute, that person is to then select from that list the trait they struggle the most with. Next, select the person most gifted in that area and have them explain how they created strength in that area, and so forth.

We would all rather share our strengths and how God has blessed us in that area. However, as Paul noted in 2 Corinthians, it is not our strengths that glorify God; instead, it is our weaknesses that give God glory. Perhaps, it is better to say that God is most glorified when we focus on eliminating the things we do poorly rather than highlighting the things we do well.

By using these gifts as a conduit for kicking in adrenalin, we can have an exponential life that others around us can only dream of. Isn't that something worth the price of admission? Taking on these and any other attributes of God will unleash God in our lives. That should make us want to get to the church building as often as possible, where other people trying to do the same will also be.

CHAPTER 19

Shock Wave Therapy

When the United States dropped atomic bombs on the cities of Hiroshima and Nagasaki, Japan in 1945, essentially ending the Second World War, the devastation from the bombs themselves was horrific. However, the power from the shock waves that emanated from the blasts caused even more destruction. At the outer edges of these after-shocks, the only houses and buildings that could have survived would have been the ones built on a strong foundation. Seeing videos of shock waves from these types of devices leaves no doubt as to the enormous force behind them. Without even touching the buildings involved, they were leveled by a power not seen by those affected. The illustration that Jesus used equating anyone not utilizing His words of wisdom to a house built upon the sand would suffer the same fate as those buildings in Japan when subjected to a similar force, just with a different magnitude. Even so, the power of shock waves is limited while the power of God is not.

Anyone who has ever had a kidney stone is probably well aware of what a shock wave is since that is one of the ways doctors can eliminate them. Some people know this procedure as lithotripsy, but most people who utilize this procedure just know that the doctor is going to bust up the stone so it won't hurt anymore. Without showing too much of my ignorance about the subject, the shock waves that emanate from the device basically pulverize the kidney stone into small pieces so they can be flushed from the body. This is done without touching the kidney but rather by focusing that energy into one area to correct the problem.

If you spend much time noticing, most people at church basically sit in the same seats each week and religiously follow the worship agenda, like they did when they were growing up. For most people, change can be hard and will be resisted, especially by those who are comfortable with their religion as long as it resembles the church of their youth. However, one thing is certain: if we keep doing what we are currently doing, we will continue to get the same results.

The church needs shock wave therapy to shake the barnacles from its foundation so it can see the problem and fix it. The best way to start this shock wave in the church is by going to the youth wing in any church and then encouraging them to raise questions about anything they don't understand. If they are too timid to raise their own questions, you can get the ball rolling by throwing out a couple of the questions that have been raised in this book or share with them some of your own. From there the shock wave or snowball will roll downhill toward a better understanding of God and why we do the things we do. Even the adults might figure out why they believe some of the things they believe by simply asking themselves out loud why they believe them. Don't be surprised that some things done in the religion of Christianity that started centuries ago have outlived their

and need to be altered. In any case, go into Scripture
~~~h approach. Try not to take any baggage with you
you open the Bible and you will find answers to any
question that may arise.

Just like lithotripsy, for the shock wave to be most effective,
its power has to be totally focused on the problem. First, we have
to acknowledge there is a problem. Second, we have to be willing
to make whatever changes are necessary for spiritual growth even
if it completely overhauls all of the rituals and rules that may have
caused the problem in the first place. Incorporating scrutiny into
our teaching curriculum will prepare people of all ages for the
spiritual assault they will face as they leave home. If we will open
the way we study the Bible to scrutiny and examination, then
something good will happen as people become more convinced
about the things they believe because they will be built on
evidence. When it is all said and done, the intention of scripture
is to help us discern how to make every next thought, decision,
or action in the direction that most resembles God's nature.

On this treasure hunt, we have been looking for items of
great value that could generate or regenerate faith in teenagers
and young adults struggling to believe. We may not have found
doubloons or pieces of eight on this journey like pirates might
have sought, but here are eight steps recapping what we have
learned on this adventure that will rekindle the fire of faith in
our youth:

1. Make the church a safe place to doubt.
2. Hit high school students with everything they will
    encounter at college so they won't be ambushed once
    they get there.

3. Set up a search and rescue mission for finding the lost faith of college students.
4. Replace rituals with spiritual exercises.
5. Make Bible lessons relevant by equating Bible stories with contemporary illustrations.
6. Demonstrate what an exponential life looks like and how to acquire it.
7. Teach young people the importance of transparency and confession as a means of killing addictions in its early stages with continual assessment of their state of faith.
8. When all else fails, show them how to serve. Nothing ignites faith in God more than serving others.

At the end of the *Wizard of Oz*, Glenda, the good witch, takes a distraught Dorothy and walks her through the things she believes and has learned during her time in Oz. As Dorothy recounts the things of great value in her life, she discovers she has had the power to access her treasure all along. It is at that point in her life that she realizes that there indeed is no place like home.

The treasure is real, and it is enormous. All it takes to access it is to believe in it, and then we will have spiritual riches untold as well as the strength and endurance to open the flood gates and bring more of God's love into it. It can never be found while going through countless and mindless rituals. It can only be accessed and unlocked when we are certain of its reality and power. How can world hunger be eliminated? How can child abuse and domestic violence be wiped off the earth? How can love flourish in the world? The answer to each of these questions is God; that is, God in us.

It is very important that we pass along to each subsequent generation a better understanding of God than was given to us. As each generation grows in strength, God's people won't be looking for the treasure as they are now. They will have found it, and every generation that follows will be able to enjoy heaven on earth. If our generation can start that ball rolling in the right direction, perhaps we can get there sooner than we think. When that happens, Jesus came and reigns. That would be something to treasure.

CPSIA information can be obtained at www.ICGtesting.com
Printed in the USA
LVOW130007300513

336035LV00001B/3/P